U.S. Department of Justice
Office of Justice Programs
Bureau of Justice Statistics

I0448437

Bureau of Justice Statistics

Special Report

January 2011, NCJ 231172

Prison Rape Elimination Act of 2003 (PREA)

Sexual Victimization Reported by Adult Correctional Authorities, 2007–2008

Paul Guerino and Allen J. Beck, Ph.D., *BJS Statisticians*

The Survey of Sexual Violence (SSV) is an annual collection based on official records that the Bureau of Justice Statistics (BJS) has conducted since 2004. It is one of a number of BJS data collections that are conducted to meet the mandates of the Prison Rape Elimination Act of 2003 (PREA).

On behalf of BJS, staff of the Governments Division of the U.S. Census Bureau mailed survey forms to correctional administrators in the Federal Bureau of Prisons, state prison systems, public and private jails, private prisons, jails in Indian country, and facilities operated by the U.S. military and Immigration and Customs Enforcement (ICE). Administrators were given the option to mail back a completed form or to complete it on the web. Data collection forms can be accessed on the BJS website at http://bjs.ojp.usdoj.gov/index.cfm?ty=dcdetail&iid=406.

Each sexual act, as defined by BJS, is classified by the perpetrator who carried out the incident (i.e., inmate or staff) and the type of act perpetrated. Administrators provided counts of the four types of sexual victimization that occurred during the prior calendar year: inmate-on-inmate nonconsensual sexual acts, inmate-on-inmate abusive sexual contacts, staff sexual misconduct, and staff sexual harassment. (See "Defining sexual victimization," page 2.)

For each type of victimization, correctional administrators indicated how many of the allegations were substantiated (determined to have occurred), unsubstantiated, unfounded (insufficient evidence to make a final determination), and still under investigation.

The administrators then completed a separate form for each substantiated allegation, providing details about the victim, perpetrator, and circumstances surrounding the incident.

Highlights

- Correctional administrators reported 7,444 allegations of sexual victimization in 2008 and 7,374 allegations in 2007.

- Total allegations of sexual victimization increased significantly between 2005 (6,241 incidents) and 2008 (7,444).

- The increase in total allegations of sexual victimization between 2005 and 2008 was largely due to prisons, where allegations increased 21%, from 4,791 incidents to 5,796.

- In 2008, 931 allegations of sexual victimization (13%) were substantiated, i.e., determined to have occurred upon investigation.

- State prison administrators reported 589 substantiated incidents of sexual violence in 2008, up 28% from 459 substantiated incidents reported in 2005.

- About 54% of substantiated incidents of sexual victimization involved only inmates, while 46% of substantiated incidents involved staff with inmates.

- Female inmates were disproportionately victimized by both other inmates and staff in federal and state prisons, as well as local jails.

- Approximately 12% of substantiated inmate-on-inmate sexual victimizations were committed by two or more perpetrators.

- Injuries were reported in about 18% of incidents of inmate-on-inmate sexual victimizations and less than 1% of incidents of staff-on-inmate sexual victimizations.

The 2007 and 2008 surveys included all federal and state prisons, facilities operated by the U.S. military and ICE, and a representative sample of jail jurisdictions and privately operated jails and prisons. The surveys also included jails holding adults in Indian country based on a complete enumeration of jails in 2008 and a representative sample of jails in 2007. In total, data were collected from facilities containing 2.12 million inmates in 2007 and 2.17 million inmates in 2008. (See *Methodology* for more information about the systems and facilities from which data were collected.)

Responses were weighted to provide national-level estimates for jails and privately operated facilities. Since the estimates for jails and privately operated facilities are based on a sample rather than a complete enumeration, they are subject to sampling error. (See *Methodology* for description of sampling procedures.)

The 2007-2008 survey results should not be used to rank systems or facilities. Given the absence of uniform reporting, caution is necessary for accurate interpretation of the survey results. Higher or lower counts among facilities may reflect variations in definitions, reporting capacities, and procedures for recording allegations, as opposed to differences in the underlying incidence of sexual victimization.

Detailed tabulations of the survey results by system and sampled facility are presented in appendix tables 19-30.

Detail on substantiated incidents

The 2008 SSV recorded 763 substantiated incidents of sexual victimization, or incidents that were investigated and determined to have occurred. Weighting this total to take into account the sampling of local jail jurisdictions, private prisons, and private jails, the estimated total number of substantiated incidents in the nation in 2008 was 931. The 2007 SSV recorded 783 substantiated incidents of sexual victimization, which when weighted represented 1,001 incidents nationwide.

For each substantiated incident reported, correctional administrators were asked to provide details on circumstances surrounding each incident, characteristics of victims and perpetrators, type of pressure or physical force, sanctions imposed, and what type of victim assistance was provided, if any. They provided detail on 97% of reported substantiated incidents. These data are displayed in tables 4–7 and appendix tables 1–18.

Defining sexual victimization

To define "sexual victimization" under the Prison Rape Elimination Act of 2003, BJS uses uniform definitions that classify each sexual act by the perpetrator who carried out the incident (i.e., inmate or staff) and the type of act perpetrated.

Inmate-on-inmate sexual victimization involves sexual contacts with a victim without his or her consent or with a victim who cannot consent or refuse. The most serious incidents, *nonconsensual sexual acts*, include—

- contact between the penis and the vagina or the penis and the anus including penetration, however slight; or

- contact between the mouth and the penis, vagina, or anus; or

- penetration of the anal or genital opening of another person by a hand, finger, or other object.

Less serious incidents, *abusive sexual contacts*, include—

- intentional touching, either directly or through the clothing, of the genitalia, anus, groin, breast, inner thigh, or buttocks of any person; and

- incidents in which the intention is to sexually exploit rather than to harm or debilitate.

Staff-on-inmate sexual victimization includes consensual or nonconsensual acts perpetrated on an inmate by an employee, volunteer, contractor, official visitor, or other agency representative. (Family, friends, and other visitors are excluded.)

Staff sexual misconduct includes any sexual behavior or act directed toward an inmate by staff, including romantic relationships. Such acts include—

- intentional touching of the genitalia, anus, groin, breast, inner thigh, or buttocks with the intent to abuse, arouse, or gratify sexual desire; or

- completed, attempted, threatened, or requested sexual acts; or

- occurrences of indecent exposure, invasion of privacy, or staff voyeurism for sexual gratification.

Staff sexual harassment includes repeated statements or comments of a sexual nature to an inmate by staff. Such statements include—

- demeaning references to an inmate's sex or derogatory comments about his or her body or clothing; or

- repeated profane or obscene language or gestures.

Summary findings

Allegations of sexual victimization

The rate of sexual victimization reported by correctional administrators increased from 3.33 incidents per 1,000 inmates in 2005 to 3.82 in 2008.

Overall, there were 7,374 allegations of sexual victimization in 2007 and 7,444 allegations in 2008 (table 1). Although there was no significant difference between the overall totals in the 2007 and 2008 collection years, total allegations of sexual victimization increased significantly between 2005 (6,241 allegations) and 2008. This increase was largely the result of increased allegations of sexual victimization in prisons, from 4,791 incidents in 2005 to 5,796 incidents in 2008. The number of allegations of sexual victimization in local and private jails did not increase by a statistically significant amount between 2005 and 2008.

The increase in the total number of reported allegations of sexual victimization corresponds with an increase in the rate of reported allegations over time, from 2.83 allegations per 1,000 inmates in 2005 to 3.18 incidents per 1,000 in 2008. As with total allegations, this trend resulted from an increase in the rate of reported allegations in prisons, from 3.33 incidents per 1,000 inmates in 2005 to 3.82 in 2008. The rate of reported allegations of sexual victimization in jails did not increase significantly between 2005 and 2008.

Allegations of inmate-on-inmate abusive sexual contacts account for two-thirds of the total increase in reported allegations of sexual victimization between 2005 and 2008.

The increase in the total number of reported allegations of sexual victimization since 2005 is due to an increase in inmate-on-inmate abusive sexual contacts. Unlike the other three types of victimization, allegations of abusive sexual contact increased significantly over time, from 611 incidents in 2005 to 1,417 in 2008 (table 2). This increase accounted for 67% of the overall increase of 1,203 allegations between 2005 and 2008.

TABLE 1
National estimates of total allegations of sexual victimization, by type of facility, 2005-2008

Facility type	Number of allegations				Rate per 1,000 inmates			
	2008*	2007	2006	2005	2008*	2007	2006	2005
Total	7,444	7,374	6,528**	6,241**	3.18	2.95	2.91**	2.83**
Prisons[a]	5,796	5,535**	4,958**	4,791**	3.82	3.62**	3.37**	3.33**
Public-federal[b]	368	309**	242**	268**	2.22	1.86**	1.50**	1.71**
Public-state	5,194	4,940**	4,516**	4,341**	4.20	3.98**	3.75**	3.68**
Jails[c]	1,633	1,823	1,533	1,406	2.04	1.89	2.02	1.86
Other adult facilities								
Indian country jails[d]	2	9**	29	32**	^	3.33**	^	^
Military-operated	6	3**	3**	8**	3.34	1.63**	1.62**	3.08**
ICE-operated	6	4**	5**	4**	0.49	0.61**	0.62**	0.61**

*Comparison group.

**Difference with comparison group is significant at the 95% confidence level.

^Too few cases to provide a reliable rate.

[a]Includes federal, state, and private prisons.

[b]Estimates for 2006 are not comparable to those in 2005 due to a change in reporting.

[c]Includes local and private jails.

[d]Excludes facilities housing juveniles only.

TABLE 2
National estimates of total allegations of sexual victimization, by type of incident, 2005–2008

Incident type	2008*	2007	2006	2005
Total	7,444	7,374	6,528**	6,241**
Inmate-on-inmate nonconsensual sexual acts	2,343	2,421	2,205	2,160
Inmate-on-inmate abusive sexual contacts	1,417	1,220**	834**	611**
Staff sexual misconduct	2,528	2,436	2,371	2,386
Staff sexual harassment	1,169	1,298	1,118	1,084**

*Comparison group.

**Difference with comparison group is significant at the 95% confidence level.

Note: Detail may not sum to total due to missing data.

BJS Surveys of Sexual Victimization in Correctional Facilities

Section 4(a)(1) of the Prison Rape Elimination Act of 2003 (PREA) requires the Bureau of Justice Statistics (BJS) to "carry out, for each calendar year, a comprehensive statistical review and analysis of the incidence and effects of prison rape" (P.L. 108-79).

BJS has developed a multiple-measure, multiple-mode data collection strategy to fully implement requirements under PREA, including three surveys relating to inmate sexual victimization. The Survey of Sexual Violence (SSV) collects administrative data annually on the incidence of sexual victimization in adult and juvenile correctional facilities. The National Inmate Survey (NIS) and the National Survey of Youth in Custody (NYSYC) gather data on the incidence of sexual assault as reported by inmates in prisons and jails and by youth held in juvenile facilities.

Substantiated incidents of sexual victimization

> State prison administrators reported an increase of 130 substantiated incidents between 2005 and 2008.

Administrators of all categories of correctional facilities reported 1,001 substantiated incidents of sexual victimization in 2007 and 931 substantiated incidents in 2008 (table 3). This change in all categories was not statistically significant, nor was the increase in substantiated incidents between 2005 (885 incidents) and 2008. State prisons experienced a 28% increase in substantiated incidents between 2005 (459 incidents) and 2008 (589 incidents). Local and private jails saw no statistically significant change during the same period.

The rate of substantiated incidents of sexual violence follows the same pattern as total substantiated incidents. While the overall rate did not change significantly between 2005 and 2008 (for both years, it was 0.4 substantiated incidents per 1,000 inmates), the rate of substantiated incidents in prisons increased from 0.36 incidents per 1,000 inmates in 2005 to 0.43 incidents per 1,000 in 2008. The rate of substantiated incidents in jails did not change significantly between 2005 and 2008.

> Substantiated incidents of inmate-on-inmate abusive sexual contacts and staff sexual harassment increased significantly between 2005 and 2008.

Substantiated incidents of inmate-on-inmate nonconsensual sexual acts declined from 326 in 2005 to 235 in 2008, but this decline was not statistically significant (table 4). Substantiated incidents of abusive sexual contacts increased significantly between 2005 and 2008, from 173 to 272. The increase in substantiated incidents of staff sexual misconduct from 338 in 2005 to 361 in 2008 was not significant. Substantiated incidents of staff sexual harassment did increase significantly, from 48 in 2005 to 63 in 2008.

TABLE 3

National estimates of substantiated incidents of sexual victimization and rates per 1,000 inmates, by type of facility 2005–2008

Facility type	Number of substantiated incidents				Rate per 1,000 inmates			
	2008*	2007	2006	2005	2008*	2007	2006	2005
Total	931	1,001	967	885	0.40	0.40	0.43	0.40
Prisons[a]	651	613	563**	524**	0.43	0.40	0.38**	0.36**
Public-federal[b]	21	14**	5**	41**	0.13	0.08**	0.03**	0.26**
Public-state	589	570**	549**	459**	0.47	0.46**	0.46**	0.39**
Jails[c]	271	380	393	348	0.34	0.39	0.52	0.46
Other adult facilities								
Indian country jails[d]	2	6	7	10	^	2.22	^	^
Military-operated	5	1**	2**	2**	2.78	0.54**	1.08**	0.77**
ICE-operated	1	1	2**	1	0.08	0.15**	0.25**	0.15**

*Comparison group.

**Difference with comparison group is significant at the 95% confidence level.

^Too few cases to provide a reliable rate.

Note: Detail may not sum to total due to rounding.

[a]Includes federal, state, and private prisons.

[b]Estimates from 2006 are not comparable to those in 2005 due to a change in reporting.

[c]Includes local and private jails.

[d]Excludes facilities housing juveniles only.

A greater percentage of allegations of abusive sexual contacts and incidents of staff sexual misconduct were substantiated in local jails than in prisons.

Administrators reported that 19% of alleged abusive sexual contacts were substantiated, as were 12% of alleged nonconsensual sexual acts, 19% of alleged incidents of staff sexual misconduct, and 5% of alleged incidents of staff sexual harassment (table 5). The percentage of substantiated allegations varied by type of facility. Local jail administrators reported substantiating a greater percentage of allegations of abusive sexual contacts (24% in jails versus 17% in prisons). Federal and state prison administrators reported that a greater percentage of allegations of inmate-on-inmate sexual victimization were found to be unsubstantiated than local jail administrators. In prisons, 63% of alleged nonconsensual sexual acts and 61% of abusive sexual contacts were unsubstantiated, while 41% of nonconsensual sexual acts and 46% of abusive sexual contacts in jails were unsubstantiated. The same was true of incidents of staff sexual misconduct: 58% of alleged incidents were found to be unsubstantiated in prisons, compared to 39% in local jails.

Incident-level findings

For each substantiated incident of sexual victimization, administrators were asked to fill out a form that collected incident-level characteristics, such as the age and sex of the victim, the number of perpetrators, any injuries to the victim, the time and location of the victimization, and sanctions imposed on the perpetrator.

TABLE 4
National estimates of total substantiated incidents of sexual victimization, by type of incident, 2005–2008

Incident type	2008*	2007	2006	2005
Total	931	1,001	967	885
Inmate-on-inmate nonconsensual sexual acts	235	268	262	326
Inmate-on-inmate abusive sexual contacts	272	218**	158**	173**
Staff sexual misconduct	361	452	471	338
Staff sexual harassment	63	63	70	48**

*Comparison group.

**Difference with comparison group is significant at the 95% confidence level.

Note: Detail may not sum to total due to rounding.

TABLE 5
National estimates of outcomes of investigations into allegations of sexual violence, by type of facility, 2007-2008

	Number of allegations			Percent by outcome[a]		
	All facilities[b]	Federal and state prisons	Local jails	All facilities[b]	Federal and state prisons*	Local jails
Inmate-on-inmate nonconsensual sexual acts	4,764	3,260	1,291	100%	100%	100%
Substantiated	503	304	161	12	11	13
Unsubstantiated	2,416	1,800	504	57	63	41**
Unfounded	1,349	739	558	32	26	46**
Investigation ongoing	495	417	69			
Inmate-on-inmate abusive sexual contacts	2,637	2,012	546	100%	100%	100%
Substantiated	490	347	132	19	17	24**
Unsubstantiated	1,508	1,209	250	58	61	46**
Unfounded	602	429	158	23	22	29
Investigation ongoing	36	27	7			
Staff sexual misconduct	4,964	3,461	1,211	100%	100%	100%
Substantiated	814	454	285	19	15	25
Unsubstantiated	2,324	1,699	443	53	58	39**
Unfounded	1,230	785	416	28	27	36
Investigation ongoing	595	523	67			
Staff sexual harassment	2,467	2,078	363	100%	100%	100%
Substantiated	126	89	33	5	4	9
Unsubstantiated	1,475	1,222	239	63	62	68
Unfounded	758	671	78	32	34	22
Investigation ongoing	108	96	12			

*Comparison group.

**Difference with comparison group is significant at the 95% confidence level.

Note: Detail may not sum to total due to missing information.

[a]Percents based on allegations for which investigations have been completed.

[b]Includes private prisons and jails, jails in Indian country, and facilities operated by the U.S. military and Immigration and Customs Enforcement (ICE).

Inmate-on-inmate sexual victimization

Females were disproportionately victimized by inmates in state and federal prisons and local jails.

Females represent 7% of sentenced prison inmates but accounted for 21% of all victims of inmate-on-inmate sexual victimization in federal and state prisons[1] (table 6). Similarly, females account for 13% of inmates in local jails but 32% of all victims.[2]

Victims and perpetrators of nonconsensual acts were more likely to be younger than 25, compared to victims and perpetrators of abusive sexual contacts.

About 42% of victims of nonconsensual sexual acts and 31% of perpetrators were younger than 25, compared to 33% of victims of abusive sexual contacts and 21% of perpetrators.

A greater percentage of perpetrators in local jails were younger than 25 compared to perpetrators in prisons. Perpetrators of inmate-on-inmate sexual victimization in local jails were more likely to be under 25 (38%) than perpetrators in prisons (17%). Perpetrators in prisons were more likely than perpetrators in local jails to be ages 25-39 (48% in prisons compared to 39% in local jails) and 40 or older (35% compared to 23%).

About 1 in 9 substantiated incidents of inmate-on-inmate sexual victimization were committed by more than one perpetrator.

Approximately 12% of substantiated incidents of inmate-on-inmate sexual victimization were committed by two or more perpetrators, but this varied by facility and incident type. Two or more perpetrators committed a greater percentage of substantiated incidents in local jails (14%) than in prisons (9%). In addition, two or more perpetrators committed a greater percentage of nonconsensual sexual acts (16%) than abusive sexual contacts (7%).

---

[1]See *Prison Inmates at Midyear 2008—Statistical Tables*, BJS Web, 8 April 2009.
[2]See *Jail Inmates at Midyear 2008—Statistical Tables*, BJS Web, 31 March 2009.

About 1 in 5 incidents of inmate-on-inmate sexual victimization resulted in a victim injury.

Under a fifth (18%) of substantiated incidents of inmate-on-inmate sexual victimization resulted in an injury. There was no significant difference in the percentage of incidents resulting in an injury in prisons compared to local jails. There was a difference by incident type: nonconsensual sexual acts were significantly more likely to result in an injury (28%) than abusive sexual contacts (8%).

Nonconsensual sexual acts were more likely than abusive sexual contacts to occur in the early morning hours (midnight to 6 a.m.). Abusive sexual contacts occurred more often during the day (6 a.m. to 6 p.m.) than nonconsensual sexual acts.

About 32% of nonconsensual sexual acts occurred between midnight and 6 a.m., compared to 12% of abusive sexual contacts. Roughly 22% of abusive sexual contacts occurred between 6 a.m. and noon (compared to 17% of nonconsensual sexual acts), and 36% occurred between noon and 6 p.m. (compared to 24% of nonconsensual sexual acts).

Solitary confinement was used most often as a sanction against perpetrators of inmate-on-inmate sexual victimization.

Solitary confinement was the most frequent sanction imposed on perpetrators of inmate-on-inmate sexual victimization, but the distribution of sanctions imposed varied by facility and incident type. Perpetrators of inmate-on-inmate sexual victimization in local jails were more likely to receive legal action (51%) than were perpetrators in prisons (26%). These legal actions included arrest (22% in jail compared to 3% in prison) and referral for prosecution (34% compared to 25%). Perpetrators of inmate-on-inmate sexual victimization were also more likely to be placed in a higher custody level within the facility (33%) in local jails compared to prisons (22%).

Perpetrators of inmate-on-inmate sexual victimization in prisons were more likely than perpetrators in local jails to be placed in solitary confinement (77% in prisons compared to 67% in jails), transferred to another facility (23% compared to 9%), receive a loss of good time or increase in bad time (22% compared to 6%), and confined to their cells (14% compared to 10%).

Sanctions were more severe for nonconsensual sexual acts than for abusive sexual contacts.

Perpetrators were subject to legal action for 41% of nonconsensual sexual acts, compared to 23% of abusive sexual contacts. They were referred for prosecution for 36% of nonconsensual sexual acts, compared to 17% of abusive sexual contacts. About 32% of nonconsensual sexual

---

TABLE 6
National estimates of selected characteristics of substantiated incidents of inmate-on-inmate sexual victimization, by type of facility and incident, 2007-2008

Characteristic	Total percent[a]	Facility type		Incident type	
		Federal and state prisons*	Local jails	Nonconsensual sexual acts*	Abusive sexual contacts
Victim characteristics					
Sex					
Male	77%	79%	68%**	92%	62%**
Female	23	21	32**	8	38**
Age					
Under 25	37%	35%	44%	42%	33%**
25-39	45	46	38	41	48**
40 or older	18	19	18	17	19
Perpetrator characteristics					
Number of perpetrators					
1	88%	91%	86%**	84%	93%**
2 or more	12	9	14**	16	7**
Sex					
Male	82%	81%	80%	93%	70%**
Female	18	19	20	7	30**
Age					
Under 25	26%	17%	38%**	31%	21%**
25-39	44	48	39**	41	47**
40 or older	30	35	23**	29	32
Incident characteristics					
Victim injured					
No	82%	83%	85%	72%	92%**
Yes	18	17	15	28	8**
Time of day[b]					
6 a.m. to noon	20%	22%	15%**	17%	22%**
Noon to 6 p.m.	30	34	23**	24	36**
6 p.m. to midnight	42	41	42	44	40
Midnight to 6 a.m.	22	19	29**	32	12**
Sanction imposed[b]					
Solitary/disciplinary	72%	77%	67%**	69%	76%**
Legal action[c]	32	26	51**	41	23**
Arrested	9	3	22**	10	8
Referred for prosecution	27	25	34**	36	17**
Confined to own cell/room	12	14	10**	11	13
Placed in higher custody within same facility	27	22	33**	32	21**
Loss of privileges	23	25	22	22	23
Transferred to another facility	22	23	9**	27	17**
Loss of good time/increase in bad time	17	22	6**	18	17
Other	14	15	12**	13	15**

*Comparison group.

**Difference with comparison group is significant at the 95% confidence level.

Note: Sex and age are reported for at most two victims in multiple-victim incidents and at most two perpetrators in multiple-perpetrator incidents. Excludes victims with unknown sex or age.

[a]Includes private prisons and jails, jails in Indian country, and facilities operated by the U.S. military and Immigration and Customs Enforcement (ICE).

[b]Detail sums to more than 100% because multiple responses were allowed for this item.

[c]Includes "given new sentence."

acts resulted in the perpetrator being placed in a higher custody level, compared to 21% of abusive sexual contacts, and 27% of the more severe acts resulted in the perpetrator being transferred to another facility, compared to 17% of abusive sexual contacts.

Staff-on-inmate sexual victimization

Females were disproportionately victimized by staff in state and federal prisons and local jails.

Following the same pattern as inmate-on-inmate sexual victimization, females account for a greater proportion of victims of staff-on-inmate victimization than they do in the overall inmate population. As previously stated, females account for 7% of sentenced prison inmates, but represent about a third of all victims of staff-on-inmate sexual victimization in federal and state prisons (32%) (table 7). Similarly, females represent only 13% of inmates in local jails but over half of all victims of staff-on-inmate victimization (56%).

Females perpetrated the majority of incidents of staff sexual misconduct, while males perpetrated the majority of incidents of staff sexual harassment.

About 61% of incidents of staff sexual misconduct and 21% of incidents of staff sexual harassment were perpetrated by females. Males perpetrated 39% of incidents of staff sexual misconduct and over three-quarters of incidents of staff sexual harassment (79%).

Over half of incidents of staff sexual harassment were reported by the victim.

In over half the incidents of staff sexual harassment (58%), the victim reported the incident to administrators, compared to 26% of the incidents of staff sexual misconduct. Incidents of staff sexual misconduct were more likely than incidents of staff sexual harassment to be reported by an individual other than the victim, including another inmate (23% of staff sexual misconduct compared to 13% of staff sexual harassment), the family of the victim (29% compared to 21%), or a correctional officer or frontline staff (8% compared to 2%). Incidents of staff sexual misconduct were also more likely than incidents of staff sexual harassment to be discovered during an unrelated investigation (4% compared to 2%) or in some other way, such as through incriminating photos or notes (15% compared to 8%).

About 2 in 5 incidents of staff-on-inmate sexual victimization occurred in a program service area.

The most common location for staff-on-inmate sexual victimization was in a program service area[3] (38%), followed by a victim's cell or room (17%), another area (17%), outside of the facility (12%), in a dormitory (10%), in a common area (10%), and in a staff area (10%). Incidents of staff sexual misconduct were more likely to occur in a staff area (11%) or another area (18%) than incidents of staff sexual harassment (6% and 10%, respectively). Incidents of staff sexual harassment were more likely to occur in a dormitory (14%) or common area (14%) than incidents of staff sexual misconduct (9% for both).

More incidents of staff sexual victimization occurred during daytime hours (6 a.m. to 6 p.m.) in federal and state prisons than in jails.

More incidents of staff-on-inmate sexual victimization occurred in federal and state prisons either between 6 a.m. and noon (45%) or noon and 6 p.m. (51%) than in local jails (21% and 36%, respectively). More incidents of staff sexual victimization occurred between 6 p.m. and midnight in local jails (51%) than in federal and state prisons (35%).

---

[3]Program service areas include the commissary, kitchen, storage area, laundry, cafeteria, workshop, and hallway.

To date, BJS has released the following reports on inmate sexual victimization in adult correctional facilities:

- Sexual Victimization in Prisons and Jails Reported by Inmates, 2008-09 (NCJ 231169)
- Sexual Victimization in Local Jails Reported by Inmates, 2007 (NCJ 221946)
- Sexual Victimization in State and Federal Prisons Reported by Inmates, 2007 (NCJ 219414)
- Sexual Violence Reported by Correctional Authorities, 2006 (NCJ 218914)
- Sexual Violence Reported by Correctional Authorities, 2005 (NCJ 214646)
- Sexual Violence Reported by Correctional Authorities, 2004 (NCJ 210333)

TABLE 7

National estimates of selected characteristics of substantiated incidents of staff sexual misconduct and harassment, by type of facility and incident, 2007-2008

Characteristic	Total percent[a]	Facility type		Incident type	
		Federal and state prisons*	Local jails	Staff sexual misconduct*	Staff sexual harassment
Victim characteristics					
Sex					
Male	63%	68%	44%**	65%	50%**
Female	37	32	56**	35	50**
Perpetrator characteristics					
Sex					
Male	44%	39%	63%**	39%	79%**
Female	56	61	37**	61	21**
Incident characteristics					
Who reported the incident[b]					
Victim	31%	27%	43%**	26%	58%**
Another inmate (non-victim)	22	23	22	23	13**
Family of victim	28	31	22	29	21**
Correctional officer/frontline staff	7	7	3**	8	2**
Anonymous	4	5	4	4	3
Discovered during unrelated investigation	4	2	2	4	2**
Other	14	14	12	15	8**
Where occurred[b]					
In victim's cell/room	17%	13%	26%**	17%	16%
In a dormitory	10	9	11	9	14**
In a common area	10	11	10	9	14**
In a program service area	38	46	14**	37	41
Outside the facility	12	12	15	13	9
Staff area	10	11	5**	11	6**
Other	17	13	28	18	10**
Time of day[b]					
6 a.m. to noon	36%	45%	21%**	36%	38%
Noon to 6 p.m.	45	51	36**	45	45
6 p.m. to midnight	40	35	51**	41	29**
Midnight to 6 a.m.	23	19	28	24	16

*Comparison group.

**Difference with comparison group is significant at the 95% confidence level.

Note: Sex and age are reported for at most two victims in multiple-victim incidents and at most two perpetrators in multiple-perpetrator incidents. Excludes victims with unknown sex or age.

[a]Includes private prisons and jails, jails in Indian country, and facilities operated by the U.S. military and Immigration and Customs Enforcement (ICE).

[b]Detail sums to more than 100% because multiple responses were allowed for this item.

Methodology

Sampling

The sampling designs for the 2007 and 2008 SSV surveys varied according to the different facilities covered under PREA. The following designs were used:

Federal and state prisons

In both 2007 and 2008, the survey included the Federal Bureau of Prisons and all 50 state adult prison systems. Prison administrators were directed to report only on incidents of sexual victimization that occurred within publicly operated adult prison facilities and to exclude incidents involving inmates held in local jails, privately operated facilities, and facilities in other jurisdictions.

Privately operated state and federal prisons

In 2007, a sample of 42 privately operated state and federal prison facilities was drawn to produce a 10% sample of the 417 private prisons identified by the *2005 Census of State and Federal Adult Correctional Facilities.* Facilities were sorted by average daily population (ADP) in the 12-month period ending June 30, 2005. Five facilities with ADPs greater than 2,145 inmates were selected with certainty because of their size.[4] The remaining facilities were sorted by region (i.e., Northeast, Midwest, South, or West), state, and ADP, and 37 facilities were sampled systematically with probability proportional to their size.[5] (See "National estimates and accuracy," page 11.)

In 2008, BJS increased the sample from 42 to 85 privately operated prison facilities with the intention of increasing the precision of private prison estimates. As in 2007, facilities were ranked by ADP in the 12-month period ending June 30, 2005. The 33 facilities with an ADP of at least 1,000 inmates were included with certainty in the 2008 SSV. The remaining facilities were sorted by region, state, and ADP, and 52 facilities were sampled systematically with probability proportional to their size.

Three privately operated prisons selected for the

---

[4]These facilities were given a 100% chance of selection in each sample because of their size.

[5]The chance of selection was directly related to the size of the facility (i.e., within each stratum, facilties with larger ADPs had a greater chance of selection than facilities with smaller ADPs).

[6]Six states have combined jail-prison systems: Alaska, Connecticut, Delaware, Hawaii, Rhode Island, and Vermont.

2008 survey closed prior to data collection:

- Pacific Furlough Facility, CA
- Horizon Center Community Corrections Center, NY
- Community Residential Treatment Services, OH.

Public jails

In 2007, a sample of 500 publicly operated jail facilities was selected based on data reported in the *2005 Census of Jail Inmates.* First, the third-largest jail jurisdiction in 44 states and the District of Columbia was selected.[6] This minimized overlap with the 2005 and 2006 studies, in which the largest and second-largest jurisdictions in those states were chosen with certainty. An additional 132 jail jurisdictions with ADPs greater than or equal to 1,000 inmates were also selected with certainty. The remaining 2,745 jail jurisdictions on the frame were then grouped into three strata. The first stratum contained 1,527 jails with an ADP of 79 or fewer inmates, the second stratum included 796 jails with an ADP of 80 to 253 inmates, and the third stratum included 422 jails with an ADP of 254 to 999 inmates. Jail jurisdictions in these three strata were sorted by region, state, and ADP and selected systematically with probability proportional to size, resulting in 72 selections from stratum one, 85 from stratum two, and 165 from stratum three.

Of the 500 selected jail jurisdictions, two did not respond to the survey:

- Marion-Walthall County Regional Correctional Facility, MS
- Desoto County Jail, MS.

Three jail jurisdictions selected for the 2007 survey closed prior to data collection:

- Haskell County Jail, TX
- Galena City Jail, KS
- Montevallo City Jail, AL.

In 2008, a sample of 500 publicly-operated jail facilities was selected based on data reported in the *2007 Deaths in Custody Annual Summary on Inmates under Jail Supervision.* First, the largest jail jurisdiction in 44 states and the District of Columbia was selected to minimize overlap with the 2006 and 2007 studies, in which the second- and third-largest jurisdictions were chosen with certainty, respectively. Another 130 jail jurisdictions with ADPs greater than or equal to 1,000 inmates were selected with certainty. The remaining 2,707 jail jurisdictions on the frame were then grouped into three strata. The first stratum contained 1,483 jails with an ADP of 84 or fewer inmates, the second stratum included 792 jails with an ADP of 85 to 263 inmates, and the third stratum included 432 jails with an ADP of 264 to 999 inmates. As in 2007, jail jurisdictions in these three strata were sorted by region, state, and ADP and selected systematically with probability proportional to their size, resulting in 63 selections from stratum one, 70 from stratum two, and 191 from stratum three.

Of the 500 selected jail jurisdictions, 6 did not respond to the survey:

- St. Clair County Jail, AL
- Welsh City Jail, LA
- Anson County Jail, NC
- Northumberland County Department of Corrections, PA
- Hudspeth County Jail, TX
- Marathon County Adult Detention, WI.

Two selected jail jurisdictions closed in 2008:

- Tyrrell County Jail, NC
- Trenton City Jail, MO.

Private jails

In 2007, a sample of 5 privately operated jails was selected based on data reported in the *2005 Census of Jail Inmates.* The 42 private facilities on the sampling frame were sorted by region, state, and ADP, and 5 jails were systematically sampled with probability proportional to size.

In 2008, a sample of 5 privately operated jails was selected based on data reported in the *2007 Deaths in Custody Annual Summary on Inmates under Jail Supervision.* Like 2007, the 41 private facilities on the sampling frame were sorted by region, state, and ADP, and 5 jails were systematically sampled with probability proportional to size.

Other correctional facilities

Three additional censuses of other correctional facilities were drawn to represent—

- all adult jails in Indian country in 2007[7]
- all facilities operated by the U.S. Air Force, U.S. Army, U.S. Navy, and U.S. Marines in the continental United States
- all facilities operated by ICE.

---

[7]A sample of 15 of the 63 adult jails in Indian country was taken in 2008 rather than a census.

Of the 66 other correctional facilities surveyed in 2007, seven did not respond to the survey:

- Fort Peck Police Department and Adult Detention, MT
- Standing Rock Law Enforcement and Adult Detention, ND
- Turtle Mountain Law Enforcement and Adult Detention, ND
- Laguna Tribal Police and Detention Center, NM
- Eastern Nevada Law Enforcement and Adult Detention, NV
- Sisseton-Wahpeton Law Enforcement and Adult Detention, SD
- ICE—Port Isabel Service Processing Center, TX.

Five of the 74 other correctional facilities surveyed in 2008 did not respond to the survey:

- Navajo Department of Corrections, Tuba City, AZ
- ICE—Krome Service Processing Center, FL
- ICE—LaSalle Detention Facility, LA
- Blackfeet Adult Detention Center, MT
- ICE—Aguadilla Service Processing Center, Puerto Rico.

Two other correctional facilities sampled for the 2007 survey closed prior to data collection:

- ICE—San Pedro Processing Center, CA
- Pine Ridge Police Department and Adult Detention, SD.

One other correctional facility sampled for the 2008 survey closed prior to data collection:

- ICE—San Pedro Processing Center, CA.

Data for each correctional system and sampled facility are displayed in appendix tables 19-30. In each table, a measure of population size has been included to provide a basis for comparing victimization counts.

Reports of sexual victimization

Since BJS first developed uniform definitions of sexual victimization, correctional administrators have significantly enhanced their abilities to report uniform data on sexual victimization. In 2008, administrators in 46 state prison systems were able to report incidents of abusive sexual contacts separately from nonconsensual sexual acts. This was an increase of 4 systems since 2006. One state limited counts of nonconsensual sexual acts to substantiated incidents, and one state limited counts of nonconsensual sexual acts to completed (versus attempted and completed) acts. The majority of state prison systems were able to report data on staff sexual misconduct using survey definitions. Three systems were unable to separate staff sexual harassment from misconduct, and one system did not track incidents of staff sexual harassment in a central database.

Public jail administrators were less likely than prison administrators to report sexual victimization based on the definitions provided. About a quarter of public jail jurisdictions did not record abusive sexual contacts separately from the more serious nonconsensual sexual acts in 2008. This is an improvement over the 2006 SSV, in which a third of public jail jurisdictions did not record this information. Ten public jail jurisdictions did not record allegations of abusive sexual contacts, 12 based counts of nonconsensual sexual acts on completed acts only, and 15 based counts of nonconsensual sexual acts on substantiated allegations only. Finally, 5 public jail jurisdictions did not keep records on allegations of nonconsensual sexual acts.

Published estimates are not adjusted to account for systems and facilities that were unable to meet BJS reporting standards. However, these systems and facilities are footnoted in appendix tables 19-30.

National estimates and accuracy

Survey responses were weighted to produce national estimates by type of correctional facility. Data from the Federal Bureau of Prisons, all state systems, 2008 jails in Indian country, military facilities, and ICE facilities received a weight of 1.00, since these systems and facilities were all selected with certainty.

Among public jails, private jails, private prisons, and 2007 jails in Indian country, facilities were assigned a weight equal to the inverse of their probability of selection. Estimates for responding public jail jurisdictions were adjusted for nonresponse by multiplying each estimate by the ratio of the total ADP in all jurisdictions within the jail's sampling stratum to the ADP among participating jurisdictions within the jail's sampling stratum.

Survey estimates for public jails, private jails, and private prisons are subject to sampling error. The estimated sampling error varies by the size of the estimate and the size of the base population.

Estimated standard errors were calculated using SUDAAN.[8] For summary statistics, the 2007 and 2008 data files were treated separately. For each file, the sampling information was retained

by treating each facility-level sample as its own stratum (or multiple strata in the case of the public jail sample), for a total of 10 strata in 2007 and 10 strata in 2008.

The 2007 and 2008 incident report data files were combined and treated as one data file. The sampling information for each year was retained by treating each facility-level sample as its own stratum (or multiple strata in the case of the public jail samples), for a total of 19 strata across both years. A finite population correction was utilized for both summary- and incident-level estimation.

Estimates of the standard errors are included in appendix tables 2, 4, 6, 8, 10, 12, 14, 16, and 18. These standard errors may be used to construct confidence intervals around survey estimates (e.g., numbers, rates, and percentages), as well as differences between these estimates. For example, the 95% confidence interval around the percentage of male victims of inmate-on-inmate sexual victimization is approximately 77% plus or minus 1.96 times 1.2% resulting in a 95% confidence interval of 74.6% to 79.4%.

Tests of statistical significance

To facilitate the analysis, rather than provide the detailed estimates for every standard error, differences in the estimates of sexual victimization for subgroups in these tables have been tested for significance at the 95% level of confidence. For example, the difference in the total number of incidents of sexual victimization in 2005 (6,241 incidents) compared to 2008 (7,444), is statistically significant at the 95% level of confidence (table 1). In all tables providing detailed comparisons, statistical differences at the 95% level of confidence have been designated with two asterisks (**). The comparison group has been designated with one asterisk (*).

Appendix tables

Appendix tables 1-6 have more detailed information on characteristics of inmate-on-inmate incidents. Characteristics of staff-on-inmate sexual victimization are described in table 5 and appendix tables 7-18. Detailed tabulations of the survey results by system and sampled facility are presented in appendix tables 19–30. All appendix tables are available on the BJS website at http://bjs.ojp.usdoj.gov/content/pub/pdf/svraca0708.pdf.

---

[8]See Research Triangle Institute (2008). *SUDAAN Language Manual Release 10.0.* Research Triangle Park, NC.

National estimates of the characteristics of victims and perpetrators in substantiated incidents of inmate-on-inmate sexual victimization, by type of facility and incident, 2007–2008

| Characteristic | Total percent[a] | Facility type | | Incident type | |
		Federal and state prisons*	Local jails	Nonconsensual sexual acts*	Abusive sexual contacts
Victim characteristics					
Number of victims					
1	96%	96%	97%**	97%	95%**
2 or more	4	4	3**	3	5**
Sex					
Male	77%	79%	68%**	92%	62%**
Female	23	21	32**	8	38**
Age					
Under 25	37%	35%	44%	42%	33%**
25-39	45	46	38	41	48**
40 or older	18	19	18	17	19
Race/Hispanic origin					
White, Non-Hispanic	73%	75%	69%	73%	73%
Black, Non-Hispanic	17	17	17	15	18
Hispanic	8	5	14**	8	8
Other, Non-Hispanic[b]	3	3	1**	3	2**
Perpetrator characteristics					
Number of perpetrators					
1	88%	91%	86%**	84%	93%**
2 or more	12	9	14**	16	7**
Sex					
Male	82%	81%	80%	93%	70%**
Female	18	19	20	7	30**
Age					
Under 25	26%	17%	38%**	31%	21%**
25-39	44	48	39**	41	47**
40 or older	30	35	23**	29	32
Race/Hispanic origin					
White, Non-Hispanic	42%	46%	33%**	39%	46%
Black, Non-Hispanic	45	44	47	47	44
Hispanic	9	6	16**	9	8
Other, Non-Hispanic[b]	4	4	4	5	3**

*Comparison group.

**Difference with comparison group is significant at the 95% confidence level.

Note: Sex, age, and race/Hispanic origin are reported for at most two victims in multiple-victim incidents and at most two perpetrators in multiple-perpetrator incidents. Excludes victims with unknown sex, age, race, or Hispanic origin.

[a]Includes private prisons and jails, jails in Indian country, and facilities operated by the U.S. military and Immigration and Customs Enforcement (ICE).

[b]Includes American Indians, Alaska Natives, Asians, Native Hawaiians, and Other Pacific Islanders.

Standard errors for appendix table 1: National estimates of the characteristics of victims and perpetrators in substantiated incidents of inmate-on-inmate sexual victimization, by type of facility and incident, 2007–2008

Characteristic	Total percent	Local jails	Incident type	
			Nonconsensual sexual acts	Abusive sexual contacts
Victim characteristics				
Number of victims				
1	0.1%	0.2%	0.1%	0.2%
2 or more	0.1	0.2	0.1	0.2
Sex				
Male	1.2%	4.2%	0.7%	1.7%
Female	1.2	4.2	0.7	1.7
Age				
Under 25	1.4%	4.5%	2.5%	1.3%
25-39	1.5	4.4	2.8	1.5
40 or older	1.2	4.1	1.1	1.9
Race/Hispanic origin				
White, non-Hispanic	1.0%	3.0%	1.5%	1.2%
Black, non-Hispanic	0.7	2.4	1.0	1.0
Hispanic	0.5	1.6	0.8	0.7
Other, non-Hispanic	0.2	0.1	0.2	0.4
Perpetrator characteristics				
Number of perpetrators				
1	1.5%	2.1%	2.9%	0.7%
2 or more	1.5	2.1	2.9	0.7
Sex				
Male	0.7%	2.2%	0.7%	1.3%
Female	0.7	2.2	0.7	1.3
Age				
Under 25	2.0%	4.7%	3.3%	1.1%
25-39	1.2	2.7	2.1	1.6
40 or older	1.4	4.2	1.5	1.8
Race/Hispanic origin				
White, Non-Hispanic	1.8%	4.6%	2.8%	1.5%
Black, Non-Hispanic	1.8	4.7	2.7	1.7
Hispanic	0.5	1.7	0.8	0.8
Other, Non-Hispanic	0.2	0.9	0.5	0.1

Note: All facilities operated by the Federal Bureau of Prisons and state prison systems were included in the survey and therefore do not have standard errors.

National estimates of the circumstances surrounding substantiated incidents of inmate-on-inmate sexual victimization, by type of facility and incident, 2007–2008

Circumstance	Total percent[a]	Facility type		Incident type	
		Federal and state prisons*	Local jails	Nonconsensual sexual acts*	Abusive sexual contacts
Type of pressure or force[b]					
None	31%	33%	32%	14%	48%**
Force/threat of force[c]	46	43	47	66	26**
Persuasion or talked into it	15	17	10**	20	9**
Other[d]	21	20	23	20	21
Victim injured					
No	82%	83%	85%	72%	92%**
Yes	18	17	15	28	8**
Where occurred[b]					
In victim's cell/room	47%	49%	42%**	57%	37%**
In a dormitory	12	10	19	11	13
In a common area	23	23	26	16	29**
In a program service area	10	11	8	4	16**
Other areas[e]	15	13	14	17	13
Time of day[b]					
6 a.m. to noon	20%	22%	15%**	17%	22%**
Noon to 6 p.m.	30	34	23**	24	36**
6 p.m. to midnight	42	41	42	44	40
Midnight to 6 a.m.	22	19	29**	32	12**
Who reported the incident[b]					
Victim	70%	66%	77%**	71%	68%
Another inmate	13	13	12	14	11
Correctional officer	21	23	16**	19	22
Other[f]	7	6	9	7	6

*Comparison group.

**Difference with comparison group is significant at the 95% confidence level.

[a]Includes private prisons and jails, jails in Indian country, and facilities operated by the U.S. military and Immigration and Customs Enforcement (ICE).

[b]Detail sums to more than 100% because multiple responses were allowed for this item.

[c]Includes "threatened with physical harm," "physically held down or restrained in some way," "physically harmed or injured," and "threatened with a weapon."

[d]Includes "bribery or blackmail," "gave victim drugs or alcohol," "offered protection from other inmates," and "other."

[e]Includes "in the perpetrator's cell/room," "in a temporary holding cell within the facility," "outside the facility," "while in transit," and "other."

[f]Includes "family of victim," "administrative staff," "medical/healthcare staff," "instructor/teacher," "counselor," "chaplain or other religious official," and "other."

APPENDIX TABLE 4

Standard errors for appendix table 3: National estimates of the circumstances surrounding substantiated incidents of inmate-on-inmate sexual victimization, by type of facility and incident, 2007–2008

			Incident type	
Circumstance	Total percent	Local jails	Nonconsensual sexual acts	Abusive sexual contacts
Type of pressure or force				
None	1.4%	4.6%	1.1%	1.7%
Force/threat of force	1.6	4.8	2.5	1.2
Persuasion or talked into it	0.5	1.5	1.2	0.4
Other	1.4	4.9	2.5	1.1
Victim injured				
No	1.5%	1.9%	2.7%	0.5%
Yes	1.5	1.9	2.7	0.5
Where occurred				
In victim's cell/room	1.3%	3.4%	2.8%	1.4%
In a dormitory	1.3	4.5	2.4	1.0
In a common area	1.3	4.6	2.4	1.2
In a program service area	1.1	4.1	0.2	2.0
Other areas	1.5	1.9	2.9	0.9
Time of day				
6 a.m. to noon	0.8%	2.5%	1.2%	1.2%
Noon to 6 p.m.	1.0	2.7	1.5	1.4
6 p.m. to midnight	1.7	5.0	3.0	1.8
Midnight to 6 a.m.	1.5	5.0	2.6	0.9
Who reported the incident				
Victim	1.0%	2.6%	1.6%	1.3%
Another inmate	0.7	2.1	1.1	0.9
Correctional officer	0.8	2.0	1.4	1.0
Other	0.5	1.9	0.7	0.8

Note: All facilities operated by the Federal Bureau of Prisons and state prison systems were included in the survey and therefore do not have standard errors.

National estimates of the sanctions imposed on perpetrators of substantiated incidents of inmate-on-inmate sexual victimization, by type of facility and incident, 2007–2008

Sanction	Total percent[a]	Facility type		Incident type	
		Federal and state prisons*	Local jails	Nonconsensual sexual acts*	Abusive sexual contacts
Solitary/disciplinary	72%	77%	67%**	69%	76%**
Legal action[b]	32	26	51**	41	23**
Arrested	9	3	22**	10	8
Referred for prosecution	27	25	34**	36	17**
Confined to own cell/room	12	14	10**	11	13
Placed in higher custody within same facility	27	22	33**	32	21**
Loss of privileges	23	25	22	22	23
Transferred to another facility	22	23	9**	27	17**
Loss of good time/increase in bad time	17	22	6**	18	17
Other[c]	14	15	12**	13	15**

*Comparison group.

**Difference with comparison group is significant at the 95% confidence level.

Note: Detail sums to more than 100% because multiple responses were allowed for this item.

[a] Includes private prisons and jails, jails in Indian country, and facilities operated by the U.S. military and Immigration and Customs Enforcement (ICE).

[b] Includes "given new sentence."

[c] Includes "given extra work" and "other."

Standard errors for appendix table 5: National estimates of the sanctions imposed on perpetrators of substantiated incidents of inmate-on-inmate sexual victimization, by type of facility and incident, 2007–2008

Sanction	Total percent	Local jails	Incident type	
			Nonconsensual sexual acts	Abusive sexual contacts
Solitary/disciplinary	1.9%	4.4%	3.4%	1.0%
Legal action	1.5	4.5	2.6	2.0
Arrested	1.2	4.3	1.1	2.2
Referred for prosecution	1.4	4.3	2.5	1.0
Confined to own cell/room	0.6	1.8	0.8	0.9
Placed in higher custody within same facility	1.6	2.0	3.1	1.9
Loss of privileges	1.3	4.3	2.2	1.1
Transferred to another facility	1.9	3.9	2.9	1.9
Loss of good time/increase in bad time	0.6	1.1	1.2	0.4
Other	0.4	1.1	0.9	0.4

Note: All facilities operated by the Federal Bureau of Prisons and state prison systems were included in the survey and therefore do not have standard errors.

APPENDIX TABLE 7

National estimates of the characteristics of substantiated incidents of staff sexual misconduct and harassment, by type of facility and incident, 2007-2008

Characteristic	Total percent[a]	Facility type	
		Federal and state prisons*	Local jails
Nature of the incident[b]			
Sexual relationship that "appeared to be willing"	62%	68%	45%**
Sexual harassment or repeated verbal statements of a sexual nature	18	19	20
Unwanted touching	8	7	9
Indecent exposure, invasion of privacy, or voyeurism for sexual gratification	4	3	5
Pressure or abuse of power resulting in a nonconsensual act	6	7	5
Physical force resulting in a sexual act	1	1	2**
Other	10	7	19**
Unknown level of coercion	3	3	3
Number of staff involved			
1	96%	98%	95%
2 or more	4	2	5
Number of victims			
1	91%	92%	91%
2 or more	9	8	9

*Comparison group.

**Difference with comparison group is significant at the 95% confidence level.

[a]Includes private prisons and jails, jails in Indian country, and facilities operated by the U.S. military and Immigration and Customs Enforcement (ICE).

[b]Detail sums to more than 100% because multiple responses were allowed for this item.

APPENDIX TABLE 8

Standard errors for appendix table 7: National estimates of the characteristics of substantiated incidents of staff sexual misconduct and harassment, by type of facility and incident , 2007-2008

Characteristic	Total percent	Local jails
Nature of the incident		
Sexual relationship that "appeared to be willing"	2.7%	7.8%
Sexual harassment or repeated verbal statements of a sexual nature	2.2	7.1
Unwanted touching	1.3	4.3
Indecent exposure, invasion of privacy or voyeurism for sexual gratification	0.6	1.6
Pressure or abuse of power resulting in a nonconsensual act	0.4	1.1
Physical force resulting in a sexual act	^	0.2
Other	1.6	5.7
Unknown level of coercion	0.4	1.2
Number of staff involved		
1	1.3%	2.0%
2 or more	1.3	2.0
Number of victims		
1	1.2%	1.9%
2 or more	1.2	1.9

^Less than 0.05.

Note: All facilities operated by the Federal Bureau of Prisons and state prison systems were included in the survey and therefore do not have standard errors.

APPENDIX TABLE 9

National estimates of circumstances surrounding substantiated incidents of staff sexual misconduct and harassment, by type of facility and incident, 2007–2008

| Circumstance | Total percent[a] | Facility type | | Incident type | |
		Federal and state prisons*	Local jails	Staff sexual misconduct*	Staff sexual harassment
Who reported the incident					
Victim	31%	27%	43%**	26%	58%**
Another inmate (non-victim)	22	23	22	23	13**
Family of victim	28	31	22	29	21**
Correctional officer/front line staff	7	7	3**	8	2**
Anonymous	4	5	4	4	3
Discovered during unrelated investigation	4	2	2	4	2**
Other	14	14	12	15	8**
Where occurred					
In victim's cell/room	17%	13%	26%**	17%	16%
In a dormitory	10	9	11	9	14**
In a common area	10	11	10	9	14**
In a program service area	38	46	14**	37	41
Outside the facility	12	12	15	13	9
Staff area	10	11	5**	11	6**
Other	17	13	28	18	10**
Time of day					
6 a.m. to noon	36%	45%	21%**	36%	38%
Noon to 6 p.m.	45	51	36**	45	45
6 p.m. to midnight	40	35	51**	41	29**
Midnight to 6 a.m.	23	19	28	24	16

*Comparison group.

**Difference with comparison group is significant at the 95% confidence level.

Note: Detail sums to more than 100% because multiple responses were allowed for each item.

[a]Includes private prisons and jails, jails in Indian country, and facilities operated by the U.S. military and Immigration and Customs Enforcement (ICE).

APPENDIX TABLE 10

Standard errors for appendix table 9: National estimates of the circumstances surrounding substantiated incidents of staff sexual misconduct and harassment, by type of facility and incident, 2007–2008

| Circumstance | Total percent | Local jails | Incident type | |
			Staff sexual misconduct	Staff sexual harassment
Who reported the incident				
Victim	2.7%	7.7%	3.2%	2.6%
Another inmate (non-victim)	1.8	5.8	2.0	1.9
Family of victim	2.0	6.0	2.3	2.0
Correctional officer/front line staff	1.2	0.9	1.4	0.1
Anonymous	0.5	1.8	0.5	2.0
Discovered during unrelated investigation	0.6	1.0	0.7	0.1
Other	1.7	4.1	1.9	1.3
Where occurred				
In victim's cell/room	1.8%	6.2%	2.1%	1.9%
In a dormitory	1.4	4.5	1.6	1.3
In a common area	1.3	4.4	1.5	1.7
In a program service area	1.7	2.4	1.9	2.2
Outside the facility	1.4	4.6	1.5	2.6
Staff area	0.8	1.5	0.9	0.3
Other	2.7	8.3	3.1	1.9
Time of day				
6 a.m. to noon	1.4%	3.4%	1.6%	2.1%
Noon to 6 p.m.	1.8	5.8	2.1	2.7
6 p.m. to midnight	2.2	6.8	2.5	2.7
Midnight to 6 a.m.	2.2	6.7	2.6	2.8

Note: All facilities operated by the Federal Bureau of Prisons and state prison systems were included in the survey and therefore do not have standard errors.

National estimates of the characteristics of victims of staff sexual misconduct and harassment, by type of facility and incident, 2007–2008

Characteristic	Total percent[a]	Facility type		Incident type	
		Federal and state prisons*	Local jails	Staff sexual misconduct*	Staff sexual harassment
Sex					
Male	63%	68%	44%**	65%	50%**
Female	37	32	56**	35	50**
Age					
Under 18	^%	^%	0%**	^%	0%**
18-24	19	13	29**	20	19
25-29	26	24	30	27	24
30-34	25	24	27	27	16**
35-39	16	20	8**	15	21**
40-44	9	12	4**	8	14**
45 or older	4	5	2**	3	7**
Race/Hispanic origin[b]					
White, non-Hispanic	55%	55%	68%**	53%	63%**
Black, non-Hispanic	33	34	27	35	26**
Hispanic	10	8	8	11	8
Other[c]	3	3	1**	3	3

*Comparison group.

**Difference with comparison group is significant at the 95% confidence level.

^Less than 0.5.

Note: Sex, age, and race/Hispanic origin are reported for at most two victims in multiple-victim incidents. Excludes victims with unknown sex, age, and/or race/Hispanic origin.

[a]Includes private prisons and jails, jails in Indian country, and facilities operated by the U.S. military and Immigration and Customs Enforcement (ICE).

[b]Detail sums to more than 100% because multiple responses were allowed for this item.

[c]Includes American Indians, Alaska Natives, Asians, Native Hawaiians, and Other Pacific Islanders.

Standard errors for appendix table 11: National estimates of the characteristics of victims of staff sexual misconduct and harassment, by type of facility and incident, 2007–2008

Characteristic	Total percent	Local jails	Incident type	
			Staff sexual misconduct	Staff sexual harassment
Sex				
Male	2.4%	7.0%	2.8%	2.3%
Female	2.4	7.0	2.8	2.3
Age				
Under 18	0.2%	0.0%	0.2%	0.0%
18-24	2.5	7.5	2.9	2.5
25-29	1.9	5.8	2.2	2.1
30-34	2.1	6.6	2.5	0.9
35-39	0.8	1.6	0.9	1.8
40-44	0.4	0.9	0.5	0.6
45 or older	0.3	0.8	0.2	1.5
Race/Hispanic origin				
White, non-Hispanic	2.0%	5.2%	2.4%	1.9%
Black, non-Hispanic	1.8	4.8	2.1	1.2
Hispanic	1.1	1.9	1.3	1.8
Other	0.2	0.1	0.3	0.1

Note: All facilities operated by the Federal Bureau of Prisons and state prison systems were included in the survey and therefore do not have standard errors.

APPENDIX TABLE 13

National estimates of the characteristics of staff involved in staff sexual misconduct and harassment, by type of facility and incident, 2007-2008

| Characteristic | Total percent[a] | Facility type | | Incident type | |
		Federal and state prisons*	Local jails	Staff sexual misconduct*	Staff sexual harassment
Sex					
Male	44%	39%	63%**	39%	79%**
Female	56	61	37**	61	21**
Age					
24 or younger	8%	6%	7%	8%	3%**
25-29	19	17	25	20	13**
30-34	15	17	10**	15	15
35-39	18	17	23	18	17
40-44	14	14	12	15	10**
45-54	21	21	22	19	28**
55 or older	5	7	2**	4	13**
Race/Hispanic origin					
White, non-Hispanic	63%	68%	55%	62%	69%
Black, non-Hispanic	24	20	29	26	13**
Hispanic	9	6	16	9	12
Other[b]	4	6	0**	3	6**

*Comparison group.

**Difference with comparison group is significant at the 95% confidence level.

Note: Sex, age, and race/Hispanic origin are reported for at most two perpetrators in multiple-perpetrator incidents. Excludes perpetrators with unknown sex, age, and/or race/Hispanic origin.

[a]Includes private prisons and jails, jails in Indian country, and facilities operated by the U.S. military and Immigration and Customs Enforcement (ICE).

[b]Includes American Indians, Alaska Natives, Asians, Native Hawaiians, and Other Pacific Islanders.

APPENDIX TABLE 14

Standard errors for appendix table 13: National estimates of the characteristics of staff involved in staff sexual misconduct and harassment, by type of facility and incident, 2007–2008

| Characteristic | Total percent | Local jails | Incident type | |
			Staff sexual misconduct	Staff sexual harassment
Sex				
Male	2.4%	6.4%	2.9%	2.1%
Female	2.4	6.4	2.9	2.1
Age				
24 or younger	1.4%	4.0%	1.6%	0.2%
25-29	2.1	6.1	2.5	2.6
30-34	1.4	2.3	1.6	2.0
35-39	1.3	4.4	1.5	1.7
40-44	1.8	4.1	2.1	0.5
45-54	2.4	7.8	2.8	3.1
55 or older	0.2	0.4	0.2	1.0
Race/Hispanic origin				
White, non-Hispanic	2.7%	7.8%	3.1%	2.8%
Black, non-Hispanic	2.3	6.6	2.7	0.7
Hispanic	2.3	7.2	2.7	3.1
Other	0.1	0.0	0.1	0.3

Note: All facilities operated by the Federal Bureau of Prisons and state prison systems were included in the survey and therefore do not have standard errors.

APPENDIX TABLE 15

National estimates of the type and position of staff involved in staff sexual misconduct and harassment, by type of facility and incident, 2007–2008

Characteristic	Total percent[a]	Facility type		Incident type	
		Federal and state prisons*	Local jails	Staff sexual misconduct*	Staff sexual harassment
Type of staff involved					
Full/part-time employee	86%	83%	93%**	86%	87%
Contract employee/vendor	13	16	5**	13	9**
Volunteer/intern	1	1	1	^	3
Other	2	1	1	2	2
Position of staff involved					
Administrator	2%	1%	5%	2%	4%
Correctional officer	65	55	82**	66	61
Clerical	2	3	2	3	0**
Maintenance or other facility support	13	17	6**	13	18**
Medical or other health care	10	12	4**	10	7**
Education staff	3	4	0**	2	4**
Other program staff	3	5	1**	3	5**
Other	4	5	3**	3	9**

*Comparison group.

**Difference with comparison group is significant at the 95% confidence level.

^Less than 0.5.

Note: Detail sums to more than 100% because multiple responses were allowed for each item.

[a]Includes private prisons and jails, jails in Indian country, and facilities operated by the U.S. military and Immigration Customs Enforcement (ICE).

APPENDIX TABLE 16

Standard errors for appendix table 15: National estimates of the type and position of staff involved in staff sexual misconduct and harassment, by type of facility and incident, 2007–2008

Characteristic	Total percent	Local jails	Incident type	
			Staff sexual misconduct	Staff sexual harassment
Type of staff involved				
Full/part-time employee	0.7%	1.4%	0.7%	2.4%
Contract employee/vendor	0.6	1.0	0.7	1.7
Volunteer/intern	0.3	1.0	0.0	2.0
Other	0.1	0.1	0.1	0.1
Position of staff involved				
Administrator	1.1%	3.8%	1.3%	1.7%
Correctional officer	1.8	4.5	2.0	2.4
Clerical	0.3	0.9	0.3	0.0
Maintenance or other facility support	0.6	1.4	0.6	1.7
Medical or other health care	0.5	1.0	0.6	0.4
Education staff	0.1	0.0	0.1	0.2
Other program staff	0.2	0.1	0.2	0.2
Other	0.3	1.0	0.1	1.9

Note: All facilities operated by the Federal Bureau of Prisons and state prison systems were included in the survey and therefore do not have standard errors.

National estimates of the impact on inmate and staff in substantiated incidents of staff sexual misconduct and harassment, by type of facility and incident, 2007–2008

Impact	Total percent[a]	Facility type		Incident type	
		Federal and state prisons*	Local jails	Staff sexual misconduct*	Staff sexual harassment
Victim injured					
No	100%	99%	100%**	100%	99%**
Yes	^	1	0**	^	1**
Medical follow-up for victim[b]					
Given medical examination	10%	11%	4%**	12%	1%**
Administered rape kit	1	2	^**	2	0**
Tested for HIV/AIDS	2	3	2	3	0**
Tested for other STDs	2	3	2	3	0**
Provided counseling or mental health treatment	15	20	5**	17	5**
None of the above	80	74	94**	77	95**
Change in housing/custody for victim[b]					
Placed in administrative segregation or protective custody	25%	24%	14%**	28%	4%**
Placed in medical unit, ward, or hospital	1	1	1	1	0**
Confined to own cell/room	2	1	^**	2	0**
Given higher level of custody in facility	2	2	0**	2	0**
Transferred to another facility	19	20	22	22	3**
Other	10	14	6**	10	9**
None of the above	51	49	65**	46	85**
Sanction imposed on staff[b]					
Legal action	45%	44%	42%	51%	9%**
Arrested	20	13	30**	23	2**
Referred for prosecution	37	41	31	42	7**
Convicted/charged/indicted	3	3	2	3	0**
Loss of job	79	78	88**	85	44**
Discharged	37	31	50**	40	23**
Staff resigned (prior to investigation)	30	34	28	32	16**
Staff resigned (after investigation)	13	15	10	14	6**
Other sanction	21	26	14**	15	60**
Reprimanded/disciplined	12	12	13	6	43**
Other[c]	12	17	4**	10	24**

*Comparison group.

**Difference with comparison group is significant at the 95% confidence level.

^Less than 0.5.

[a]Includes private prisons and jails, jails in Indian country, and facilities operated by the U.S. military and Immigration Customs Enforcement (ICE).

[b]Detail sums to more than 100% because multiple responses were allowed.

[c]Includes "demoted/diminished responsibilities," "transferred to another facility," and "other."

APPENDIX TABLE 18

Standard errors for appendix table 17: National estimates of the impact on inmate and staff in substantiated incidents of staff sexual misconduct and harassment, by type of facility and incident, 2007–2008

Impact	Total percent	Local jails	Incident type	
			Staff sexual misconduct	Staff sexual harassment
Victim injured				
No	^%	0.0%	^%	^%
Yes	^	0.0	^	^
Medical follow-up for victim				
Given medical examination	1.2%	1.0%	1.4%	0.0%
Administered rape kit	0.1	^	0.1	0.0
Tested for HIV/AIDS	0.3	0.9	0.3	0.0
Tested for other STDs	0.3	0.9	0.3	0.0
Provided counseling or mental health treatment	0.6	1.0	0.8	1.3
None of the above	1.3	1.1	1.5	1.2
Change in housing/custody for victim				
Placed in administrative segregation or protective custody	1.9%	5.0%	2.1%	0.2%
Placed in medical unit, ward, or hospital	^	0.1	^	0.0
Confined to own cell/room	0.4	^	0.4	0.0
Given higher level of custody in facility	0.1	0.0	0.1	0.0
Transferred to another facility	2.0	6.7	2.4	0.2
Other	0.4	0.6	0.4	0.4
None of the above	2.3	6.9	2.7	0.7
Sanction imposed on staff				
Legal action	2.5%	7.6%	2.9%	0.4%
Arrested	2.5	7.2	2.9	0.1
Referred for prosecution	2.3	7.2	2.8	0.4
Convicted/charged/indicted	0.3	0.9	0.4	0.0
Loss of job	1.5	2.4	1.8	2.6
Discharged	2.7	7.9	3.0	2.8
Staff resigned (prior to investigation)	2.2	6.9	2.5	1.9
Staff resigned (after investigation)	1.3	4.0	1.5	0.3
Other sanction	1.4	4.6	1.6	2.7
Reprimanded/disciplined	1.4	4.6	1.6	2.4
Other	0.5	0.9	0.5	1.5

^Less than 0.5.

Note: All facilities operated by the Federal Bureau of Prisons and state prison systems were included in the survey and therefore do not have standard errors.

Allegations of inmate-on-inmate sexual victimization reported by federal and state prison authorities, by year and type of victimization, 2007–2008

Jurisdiction	Prisoners in custody, 6/30/2008[a]	2008 Reported inmate-on-inmate nonconsensual sexual acts		2008 Reported inmate-on-inmate abusive sexual contacts		2007 Reported inmate-on-inmate nonconsensual sexual acts		2007 Reported inmate-on-inmate abusive sexual contacts	
		Allegations	Substantiated	Allegations	Substantiated	Allegations	Substantiated	Allegations	Substantiated
Total	1,405,074	1,577	136	1,105	193	1,683	168	907	154
Federal	165,690	74	1	30	2	19	0	9	0
State									
Alabama[b]	24,861	47	1	4	0	11	0	/	/
Alaska[b,c]	3,796	0	0	/	/	0	0	/	/
Arizona	31,345	58	1	19	1	63	0	26	1
Arkansas	13,235	5	2	11	5	13	5	10	4
California	169,532	113	4	31	7	117	6	12	2
Colorado	17,720	31	7	13	2	50	13	34	6
Connecticut	20,590	27	2	22	0	22	2	16	0
Delaware	7,200	1	0	0	0	4	0	2	0
Florida	89,102	148	0	31	0	171	0	31	0
Georgia[b,c]	48,870	68	0	/	/	70	1	/	/
Hawaii[c]	3,398	6	1	/	/	1	1	0	0
Idaho	5,387	2	2	3	2	1	1	5	5
Illinois	45,548	17	2	2	0	29	2	7	1
Indiana	23,762	25	2	13	0	19	1	11	1
Iowa	8,740	26	7	58	16	31	10	58	16
Kansas	8,653	31	1	21	3	28	1	18	2
Kentucky	12,846	15	5	7	1	10	3	6	0
Louisiana	20,929	39	8	14	1	21	1	4	0
Maine	2,163	1	1	4	4	1	0	5	4
Maryland[c]	22,956	21	1	/	/	17	1	0	0
Massachusetts	11,346	23	12	32	16	18	8	21	5
Michigan[d]	50,482	22	7	30	18	21	3	29	22
Minnesota	7,820	23	1	2	0	17	0	9	2
Mississippi[b,e]	12,899	5	0	0	0	7	0	/	/
Missouri	30,004	45	2	11	2	37	3	14	5
Montana	1,629	36	4	8	6	18	6	5	1
Nebraska	4,478	5	0	9	4	5	1	10	2
Nevada	13,006	16	1	15	3	34	0	10	0
New Hampshire[b]	2,890	7	0	2	0	29	0	/	/
New Jersey	22,605	5	0	8	1	13	1	2	0
New Mexico	3,446	4	0	1	0	0	0	0	0
New York	62,019	23	1	18	3	37	6	24	7
North Carolina	39,326	58	5	35	7	38	13	47	3
North Dakota	1,425	0	0	3	1	3	1	3	3
Ohio	48,230	64	16	22	9	67	12	25	15
Oklahoma	18,034	28	0	9	2	46	3	1	0
Oregon	13,499	17	0	7	2	20	4	2	0
Pennsylvania	44,957	33	8	23	4	42	6	9	2
Rhode Island	3,890	6	2	8	7	3	0	7	4
South Carolina[f]	24,492	2	2	1	1	0	0	0	0
South Dakota	3,320	5	0	4	1	5	1	7	2
Tennessee	14,357	20	0	9	4	35	3	6	1
Texas	140,054	210	2	416	4	261	3	327	3
Utah	5,153	15	3	24	3	8	3	27	0
Vermont	1,579	20	7	39	29	20	6	27	17

Allegations of inmate-on-inmate sexual victimization reported by federal and state prison authorities, by year and type of victimization, 2007–2008

| | | 2008 | | | | 2007 | | | |
| | Prisoners in custody, 6/30/2008[a] | Reported inmate-on-inmate nonconsensual sexual acts | | Reported inmate-on-inmate abusive sexual contacts | | Reported inmate-on-inmate nonconsensual sexual acts | | Reported inmate-on-inmate abusive sexual contacts | |
Jurisdiction		Allegations	Substantiated	Allegations	Substantiated	Allegations	Substantiated	Allegations	Substantiated
State (continued)									
Virginia	32,195	38	2	15	4	25	3	1	1
Washington	17,055	45	10	17	4	110	22	14	6
West Virginia	4,959	2	1	7	4	2	2	0	0
Wisconsin	22,378	36	0	43	10	51	5	23	9
Wyoming	1,224	9	2	4	0	13	5	3	2

/Not reported.

[a]Excludes inmates in privately-operated facilities and facilities operated and administered by local governments. Counts were based on National Prisoners Statistics (NPS-1A), 2008.

[b]Allegations of abusive sexual contacts could not be counted separately from allegations of nonconsensual sexual acts in 2007.

[c]Allegations of abusive sexual contacts could not be counted separately from allegations of nonconsensual sexual acts in 2008.

[d]Counts of nonconsensual sexual acts limited to completed acts only in 2008.

[e]Counts of nonconsensual sexual acts limited to completed acts only in 2007.

[f]Counts of nonconsensual sexual acts limited to substantiated incidents only in 2007 and 2008.

APPENDIX TABLE 20

Allegations of staff-on-inmate sexual victimization reported by federal and state prison authorities, by year and type of victimization, 2007–2008

Jurisdiction	2008				2007			
	Reported allegations of staff sexual misconduct with inmates		Reported allegations of staff sexual harassment of inmates		Reported allegations of staff sexual misconduct with inmates		Reported allegations of staff sexual harassment of inmates	
	Allegations	Substantiated	Allegations	Substantiated	Allegations	Substantiated	Allegations	Substantiated
Total	1,818	233	1,062	48	1,643	221	1,016	41
Federal	161	10	103	8	182	8	99	6
State								
Alabama	23	2	4	0	5	1	3	1
Alaska[a,b]	0	0	/	/	0	0	/	/
Arizona	61	7	3	3	50	7	0	0
Arkansas	20	6	17	0	8	4	27	3
California	28	1	0	0	17	1	14	0
Colorado	14	1	2	2	32	13	5	0
Connecticut	1	0	2	0	2	0	1	0
Delaware	8	1	0	0	0	0	1	0
Florida	150	1	210	1	130	2	191	2
Georgia	78	3	29	0	85	3	0	0
Hawaii	0	0	1	0	3	0	1	0
Idaho	5	5	0	0	3	1	0	0
Illinois	26	4	0	0	29	8	0	0
Indiana	37	6	7	1	14	5	4	0
Iowa	49	8	19	4	53	11	23	4
Kansas	37	7	16	3	22	5	8	2
Kentucky	8	4	0	0	15	9	0	0
Louisiana	47	2	117	0	55	4	37	0
Maine	6	6	0	0	1	0	0	0
Maryland[b]	19	0	/	/	27	1	0	0
Massachusetts	28	5	8	0	68	4	6	0
Michigan	34	1	321	7	20	2	429	6
Minnesota	12	1	1	0	7	0	0	0
Mississippi[a]	1	1	0	0	5	0	/	/
Missouri	55	11	11	1	69	10	11	1
Montana	18	2	5	0	9	2	0	0
Nebraska	14	0	12	0	18	1	10	1
Nevada	20	3	10	1	8	0	4	0
New Hampshire	1	0	1	0	4	0	0	0
New Jersey	8	2	2	0	2	1	1	0
New Mexico	3	0	0	0	1	0	0	0
New York	224	13	39	5	161	8	51	3
North Carolina	101	19	38	0	58	11	16	1
North Dakota	2	0	0	0	0	0	0	0
Ohio	50	7	4	0	67	15	9	0
Oklahoma	29	12	5	0	24	6	3	1
Oregon	17	1	4	1	17	3	1	1
Pennsylvania	46	5	33	0	30	9	15	2
Rhode Island[a,b]	7	1	/	/	5	1	/	/
South Carolina	5	5	0	0	2	2	0	0
South Dakota	4	1	0	0	4	0	0	0
Tennessee	18	9	1	0	13	7	8	1
Texas[c]	129	4	/	/	123	8	/	/
Utah	5	1	0	0	5	0	1	0
Vermont	23	8	12	5	24	6	9	4

Allegations of staff-on-inmate sexual victimization reported by federal and state prison authorities, by year and type of victimization, 2007–2008

| | 2008 | | | | 2007 | | | |
| | Reported allegations of staff sexual misconduct with inmates | | Reported allegations of staff sexual harassment of inmates | | Reported allegations of staff sexual misconduct with inmates | | Reported allegations of staff sexual harassment of inmates | |
Jurisdiction	Allegations	Substantiated	Allegations	Substantiated	Allegations	Substantiated	Allegations	Substantiated
State (continued)								
Virginia	30	7	1	0	33	10	2	0
Washington	93	21	9	1	51	13	6	0
West Virginia	13	12	2	2	12	11	0	0
Wisconsin	48	6	12	2	66	4	19	1
Wyoming	2	1	1	1	4	4	1	1

/Not reported.

aAllegations of staff sexual harassment could not be counted separately from allegations of staff sexual misconduct in 2007.

bAllegations of staff sexual harassment could not be counted separately from allegations of staff sexual misconduct in 2008.

cJurisdiction did not record allegations of staff sexual harassment in 2007 and 2008.

Allegations of inmate-on-inmate sexual violence reported by local jail authorities, by year and type of violence, 2007–2008

Jurisdiction and facility	2008 Average daily population	Reported inmate-on-inmate nonconsensual sexual acts Allegations	Substantiated	Reported inmate-on-inmate abusive sexual contacts Allegations	Substantiated	2007 Average daily population	Reported inmate-on-inmate nonconsensual sexual acts Allegations	Substantiated	Reported inmate-on-inmate abusive sexual contacts Allegations	Substantiated
Total	/	517	44	196	49	/	455	71	178	45
Alabama										
Calhoun Co.[a,b]	343	0	0	/	/	400	1	1	/	/
Etowah Co. Det. Ctr.[b]	812	3	1	/	/	~	~	~	~	~
Jefferson Co.[b]	1,099	2	0	0	0	1,212	5	1	0	0
Morgan Co. & Annex	~	~	~	~	~	270	0	0	1	0
Arizona										
Maricopa Co.[a]	9,249	6	3	6	3	9,241	15	7	/	/
Pima Co. Adult Det. Ctr.	1,921	0	0	1	0	1,891	0	0	0	0
Arkansas										
Craighead Co. Det. Ctr.	311	1	1	0	0	~	~	~	~	~
Faulkner Co. Det. Ctr.[c,d,e]	373	1	0	0	0	325	0	0	0	0
Sebastian Co. Adult Det. Ctr.	~	~	~	~	~	381	1	0	0	0
California										
Alameda Co.	4,431	6	1	1	1	4,278	4	0	0	0
Contra Costa Co.[a]	1,612	1	0	0	0	1,600	0	0	/	/
Fresno Co.[a]	2,961	1	1	1	1	2,861	2	1	/	/
Kern Co.	2,260	0	0	1	1	2,392	1	0	0	0
Los Angeles Co. - Custody Support Svs.[a,b]	19,569	13	1	/	/	19,374	12	12	/	/
Madera Co.[c]	350	2	0	0	0	~	~	~	~	~
Orange Co.[b]	6,178	1	0	/	/	6,360	0	0	0	0
Riverside Co.	3,481	3	0	2	0	3,521	3	3	1	1
Sacramento Co.	4,575	1	1	1	1	2,139	2	2	0	0
San Diego Co.	5,184	1	0	1	1	5,072	0	0	3	2
San Francisco City & Co.[a]	2,086	2	0	2	0	2,011	8	0	/	/
San Joaquin Co.[a]	1,500	2	0	1	0	1,566	0	0	/	/
San Mateo Co.[a]	1,125	0	0	0	0	1,198	2	0	/	/
Santa Clara Co.[a]	4,610	6	2	0	0	4,640	4	2	/	/
Solano Co.[b]	937	1	0	/	/	1,065	0	0	0	0
Sonoma Co.	1,027	0	0	3	3	1,056	0	0	0	0
Stanislaus Co.	1,339	0	0	0	0	1,368	1	0	0	0
Tulare Co.	1,529	0	0	0	0	1,527	0	0	1	1
Ventura Co.	835	1	1	0	0	850	0	0	1	1
Colorado										
Arapahoe Co.	1,171	2	1	2	0	1,352	7	4	2	2
Denver Co.[b,f]	2,281	4	2	/	/	2,395	20	2	/	/
El Paso Co.	1,538	0	0	3	3	1,522	0	0	1	1
Jefferson Co.[f]	1,182	0	0	0	0	1,302	3	1	/	/
Larimer Co. Det. Ctr.	463	0	0	1	0	537	0	0	0	0
Mesa Co. Det. Fac.[b]	347	1	0	/	/	368	0	0	0	0
Weld Co.	690	0	0	5	1	~	~	~	~	~
Florida										
Alachua Co.[b]	910	1	0	/	/	1,079	0	0	0	0
Brevard Co. Det. Ctr.	1,812	1	1	3	1	1,797	4	0	5	0
Broward Co.	5,364	1	0	0	0	5,305	0	0	2	0
Collier Co.	1,138	0	0	0	0	1,224	2	0	0	0
Escambia Co.	1,812	0	0	2	0	1,881	1	0	1	0
Hillsborough Co.[a,b]	3,847	4	0	/	/	4,015	2	1	/	/
Jacksonville City	3,727	8	1	6	0	3,629	8	3	5	0
Leon Co. Det. Fac.	1,132	1	0	0	0	1,153	0	0	0	0
Manatee Co.	1,294	3	0	0	0	1,423	19	0	0	0
Marion Co.	1,832	0	0	0	0	2,007	1	0	1	0
Miami-Dade Co. Corr. & Rehab.	7,013	14	0	2	0	6,975	5	0	1	0
Okeechobee Co.	263	1	0	0	0	~	~	~	~	~
Orange Co.	4,454	4	2	2	1	4,096	0	0	0	0

Allegations of inmate-on-inmate sexual violence reported by local jail authorities, by year and type of violence, 2007-2008

Jurisdiction and facility	2008 Average daily population	2008 Reported inmate-on-inmate nonconsensual sexual acts Allegations	Substantiated	2008 Reported inmate-on-inmate abusive sexual contacts Allegations	Substantiated	2007 Average daily population	2007 Reported inmate-on-inmate nonconsensual sexual acts Allegations	Substantiated	2007 Reported inmate-on-inmate abusive sexual contacts Allegations	Substantiated
Florida (continued)										
Palm Beach Co.[b]	2,980	5	0	/	/	2,555	2	0	0	0
Pasco Co.	1,277	1	0	0	0	1,271	1	0	0	0
Pinellas Co.[f]	3,368	3	1	0	0	3,593	8	0	/	/
Polk Co.	2,374	1	0	2	0	2,466	14	0	3	0
Sarasota Co.[b,d,g]	1,019	1	0	/	/	1,045	0	0	0	0
Seminole Co. Corr. Fac.	1,003	3	0	0	0	~	~	~	~	~
St. Lucie Co. Main Jail	1,550	6	0	1	0	1,434	2	0	2	0
Volusia Co.	1,383	3	0	0	0	1,533	0	0	0	0
Georgia										
Carroll Co.[a,d,g]	~	~	~	~	~	533	1	0	/	/
Chatham Co. Adult Det. Ctr.[a,d,g]	1,739	0	0	1	0	1,718	0	0	/	/
Cobb Co. Sheriff's Office Jail & Prison Unit[a]	2,490	1	1	0	0	2,104	4	1	/	/
Dougherty Co.	831	0	0	1	0	816	0	0	0	0
Fulton Co.[b]	2,846	0	0	/	/	2,834	5	0	7	0
Gordon Co.	249	0	0	1	1	~	~	~	~	~
Gwinnett Co.[a]	2,691	3	0	0	0	2,478	0	0	/	/
Muscogee Co.[b]	565	3	0	/	/	~	~	~	~	~
Walton Co.[a]	419	0	0	0	0	371	1	1	/	/
Ware Co.	383	3	1	~	~	~	~	~	~	~
Idaho										
Ada Co.	980	1	0	2	1	920	0	0	4	1
Canyon Co.[b]	479	1	0	/	/	~	~	~	~	~
Kootenai Co.[a]	~	~	~	~	~	379	1	1	/	/
Twin Falls Co.[b]	203	124	0	/	/	~	~	~	~	~
Illinois										
Cook Co. - Dept. of Corr.	9,355	14	1	0	0	9,600	10	0	2	0
Kane Co.	671	0	0	0	0	615	0	0	1	0
Winnebago Co.	758	1	0	~	~	665	4	1	1	0
Indiana										
Elkhart Co. Security Ctr. (Jail)[b]	747	2	1	/	/	~	~	~	~	~
Hamilton Co.	~	~	~	~	~	327	0	0	2	0
Lake Co.[e]	923	0	0	1	1	937	0	0	0	0
St. Joseph Co.	650	2	0	0	0	~	~	~	~	~
Vanderburgh Co.[f]	~	~	~	~	~	708	1	0	/	/
Vigo Co.[b]	290	1	0	/	/	~	~	~	~	~
Kansas										
Chautauqua Co.[a]	~	~	~	~	~	9	1	0	/	/
Sedgwick Co.	1,553	0	0	6	0	1,522	1	0	3	0
Shawnee Co. Adult Det. Division	~	~	~	~	~	475	1	0	4	1
Kentucky										
Campbell Co.[b]	425	1	1	/	/	427	0	0	0	0
Clark Co. Det.[a]	~	~	~	~	~	8	1	0	/	/
Daviess Co. Det. Ctr.[a]	~	~	~	~	~	614	3	0	/	/
Franklin Co. Reg. Jail[d]	~	/ ~	~	~	~	319	1	1	4	0
Henderson Co. Det. Ctr.[b,e]	547	0	0	/	/	496	0	0	8	0
Lexington-Fayette Co. Det. Div.[b,e]	1,237	2	0	/	/	1,252	0	0	0	0
Louisville Metropolitan Dept. of Corr.[b]	1,902	5	0	/	/	1,810	1	0	0	0

Allegations of inmate-on-inmate sexual violence reported by local jail authorities, by year and type of violence, 2007-2008

| | 2008 | | | | | 2007 | | | | |
| | Average daily population | Reported inmate-on-inmate nonconsensual sexual acts | | Reported inmate-on-inmate abusive sexual contacts | | Average daily population | Reported inmate-on-inmate nonconsensual sexual acts | | Reported inmate-on-inmate abusive sexual contacts | |
Jurisdiction and facility		Allegations	Substantiated	Allegations	Substantiated		Allegations	Substantiated	Allegations	Substantiated
Louisiana										
Avoyelles Parish	1,231	0	0	0	0	1,230	1	1	0	0
Bossier Parish[h]	1,262	1	0	0	0	~	~	~	~	~
East Baton Rouge Prison	1,671	3	0	4	0	1,606	4	0	3	0
Jefferson Parish Jail	~	~	~	~	~	839	0	0	1	1
Lafayette Parish Jail	~	~	~	~	~	1,090	1	0	2	0
New Orleans Parish Prison System	2,570	7	0	0	0	2,685	3	1	0	0
Richland Parish Det. Ctr.[b]	854	0	0	/	/	840	2	0	0	0
Sherman Walker Corr. Ctr.	~	~	~	~	~	298	2	0	0	0
St. Landry Parish Jail	~	~	~	~	~	23	2	0	0	0
Terrebonne Parish Jail	670	1	0	0	0	~	~	~	~	~
Maine										
Cumberland Co.	402	2	0	0	0	462	0	0	0	0
Kennebec Co.	~	~	~	~	~	170	1	0	0	0
Maryland										
Anne Arundel Co.	1,128	5	0	2	0	1,123	0	0	3	3
Baltimore City[b]	4,113	5	1	/	/	3,899	9	0	0	0
Baltimore Co. Bureau of Corr.	1,360	2	0	4	3	1,356	5	3	0	0
Caroline Co.	~	~	~	~	~	100	1	0	0	0
Montgomery Co.	~	~	~	~	~	998	3	0	3	0
Massachusetts										
Barnstable Co. Jail & House of Corr.[a]	416	1	0	2	0	440	2	1	/	/
Bristol Co.	1,483	3	0	7	3	1,472	4	0	3	1
Essex Co. Corr. Fac.	1,624	1	0	0	0	1,631	2	1	0	0
Hampden Co.[a]	1,911	3	0	0	0	2,138	6	0	/	/
Hampshire Co. Jail & House of Corr.	288	1	1	1	1	~	~	~	~	~
Middlesex Co. Jail & House of Corr.	1,294	4	0	0	0	1,326	0	0	1	0
Norfolk Co.[a]	~	~	~	~	~	702	2	0	/	/
Suffolk Co.	711	0	0	1	0	698	0	0	0	0
Suffolk Co. House of Corr.[a]	1,733	4	1	11	1	1,685	8	0	/	/
Worcester Co. Jail & House of Corr.[a]	1,282	6	1	0	0	1,415	4	0	/	/
Michigan										
Berrien Co.	363	0	0	5	1	388	0	0	6	1
Kent Co.[a]	1,307	0	0	1	1	1,352	0	0	/	/
Macomb Co.[a]	1,361	1	0	4	2	1,398	2	1	/	/
Oakland Co.	1,814	0	0	6	0	1,961	0	0	4	3
St. Joseph Co.	269	0	0	1	0	~	~	~	~	~
Wayne Co.[a,b]	2,185	10	0	/	/	2,713	2	1	/	/
Minnesota										
Nobles Co.[a]	~	~	~	~	~	57	1	0	/	/
Mississippi										
Harrison Co.	1,160	0	0	0	0	1,150	8	1	0	0
Missouri										
Franklin Co.[b]	121	1	1	/	/	~	~	~	~	~
Greene Co.[c]	539	1	0	1	0	~	~	~	~	~
St. Louis Co. - Dept. of Justice Services[b]	1,186	2	0	0	0	~	~	~	~	~
Montana										
Cascade Co. Reg. Jail	380	1	1	0	0	~	~	~	~	~
Missoula Co.[a]	314	1	0	0	0	337	0	0	/	/
Nebraska										
Douglas Dept. of Corr.	1,148	0	0	0	0	1,041	2	0	1	1
Lancaster Co.	450	0	0	0	0	474	0	0	2	2

Allegations of inmate-on-inmate sexual violence reported by local jail authorities, by year and type of violence, 2007-2008

| | 2008 | | | | | 2007 | | | | |
| | Average daily population | Reported inmate-on-inmate nonconsensual sexual acts | | Reported inmate-on-inmate abusive sexual contacts | | Average daily population | Reported inmate-on-inmate nonconsensual sexual acts | | Reported inmate-on-inmate abusive sexual contacts | |
Jurisdiction and facility		Allegations	Substantiated	Allegations	Substantiated		Allegations	Substantiated	Allegations	Substantiated
Nevada										
Clark Co. Det. Ctr.	3,061	6	0	0	0	3,745	4	0	2	0
Washoe Co. Det. Ctr.[b]	1,048	0	0	/	/	1,200	0	0	7	3
North Las Vegas Det. Corr. Ctr.	~	~	~	~	~	869	1	0	1	1
New Hampshire										
Hillsborough Co. House of Corr.	583	1	0	0	0	~	~	~	~	~
Strafford Co.	~	~	~	~	~	405	1	0	0	0
New Jersey										
Atlantic Co. Jail - Dept. of Public Safety[a]	914	1	0	0	0	909	6	3	/	/
Camden Co. Corr. Fac.[b]	1,640	4	0	/	/	1,608	0	0	0	0
Cumberland Co.	580	1	0	0	0	~	~	~	~	~
Essex Co. Corr. Fac.[b]	2,332	1	0	/	/	3,028	0	0	0	0
Hudson Co. Corr. Fac.	1,885	4	0	0	0	1,946	4	1	1	0
Mercer Co. Corr. Ctr.[b]	995	1	0	/	/	~	~	~	~	~
Middlesex Co. Adult Corr. Ctr.[a]	1,204	3	0	0	0	980	3	2	/	/
Monmouth Co. Corr. Inst.	977	1	0	2	0	1,209	3	0	0	0
Passaic Co.[a]	1,509	1	0	0	0	1,912	1	0	/	/
Union Co.	8,085	1	0	0	0	1,070	2	0	0	0
New Mexico										
Bernalillo Co./City Det. Ctr.	5,483	2	0	1	0	2,613	7	0	0	0
New York										
Albany Co. Corr. Fac.	687	0	0	2	0	762	0	0	0	0
Erie Co. Holding Ctr.[b]	1,364	1	0	/	/	~	~	~	~	~
Erie Couny Corr. Fac.	~	~	~	~	~	1,469	0	0	1	1
New York City	13,546	11	0	2	0	14,064	6	0	4	0
Schenectady Co.	305	0	0	0	0	317	3	0	0	0
North Carolina										
Gaston Co.	541	0	0	0	0	517	1	1	0	0
Mecklenburg Co.[b]	2,578	1	0	/	/	2,585	0	0	1	0
North Dakota										
Grand Forks Co. Corr. Ctr.[b]	171	3	1	/	/	159	0	0	1	0
Ohio										
Butler Co.	1,042	1	0	0	0	1,101	0	0	0	0
Cuyahoga Co. Corr. Ctr.	1,941	1	0	5	0	1,978	3	0	6	1
Franklin Co.	2,202	4	0	0	0	2,314	0	0	0	0
Hamilton Co.[d]	2,019	3	0	0	0	2,086	0	0	2	2
Lorain Co.[a]	427	0	0	2	1	450	1	0	/	/
Muskingum Co.	~	~	~	~	~	154	1	0	0	0
Oklahoma										
Oklahoma Co.[a]	2,281	7	0	6	0	2,369	5	1	/	/
Oregon										
Deschutes Co. Corr. Fac.	201	0	0	2	0	210	0	0	3	0
Marion Co.[b]	501	1	0	/	/	~	~	~	~	~
Multnomah Co. Det. Fac.	1,502	4	0	5	0	1,592	10	0	2	0
Pennsylvania										
Allegheny Co.[a]	2,749	7	3	0	0	2,650	0	0	/	/
Berks Co. Prison	1,109	0	0	0	0	1,304	2	1	4	3
Bucks Co.	780	1	0	1	0	1,180	0	0	1	1
Dauphin Co. Prison	~	~	~	~	~	979	1	0	0	0
Franklin Co. Prison[a]	358	0	0	0	0	343	2	0	/	/
Lancaster Co. Prison[a]	1,160	1	0	0	0	1,197	3	0	/	/
Lehigh Co.	1,169	0	0	1	0	1,181	5	0	3	0
Montgomery Co. Prison Corr. Fac.	1,742	0	0	0	0	1,614	1	0	0	0

Allegations of inmate-on-inmate sexual violence reported by local jail authorities, by year and type of violence, 2007-2008

| | 2008 | | | | | 2007 | | | | |
| | Average daily population | Reported inmate-on-inmate nonconsensual sexual acts | | Reported inmate-on-inmate abusive sexual contacts | | Average daily population | Reported inmate-on-inmate nonconsensual sexual acts | | Reported inmate-on-inmate abusive sexual contacts | |
Jurisdiction and facility		Allegations	Substantiated	Allegations	Substantiated		Allegations	Substantiated	Allegations	Substantiated
Pennsylvania (continued)										
Northampton Co. Dept. of Corr.[b]	779	3	0	/	/	906	0	0	0	0
Philadelphia Prison System[b]	9,287	4	0	0	0	10,200	11	0	0	0
York Co. Prison[b]	2,172	1	0	0	0	2,031	0	0	0	0
South Carolina										
Charleston Co.[a,b]	1,694	0	0	/	/	1,762	2	0	/	/
South Dakota										
Minnehaha Co.	520	1	1	0	0	520	0	0	0	0
Tennessee										
Blount Co.[a]	~	~	~	~	~	394	1	0	/	/
Davidson Co. Sheriff's Office	2,470	2	0	4	3	2,470	6	1	7	1
Rutherford Co.	771	1	0	0	0	~	~	~	~	~
Shelby Co. Corr. Ctr.[a,b]	2,960	4	0	/	/	2,960	5	0	/	/
Shelby Co. Justice Ctr.	2,678	1	0	0	0	2,733	5	0	0	0
Texas										
Bexar Co. Adult Det. Ctr.[a]	4,211	6	2	6	4	3,176	9	0	/	/
Collin Co.	897	1	0	0	0	~	~	~	~	~
Dallas Co.[a,b,e]	6,157	4	0	/	/	7,180	1	0	/	/
Ector Co.[a,b,g]	583	0	0	/	/	594	1	0	/	/
El Paso Co. Det. Fac.[a,b]	2,209	0	0	/	/	2,220	1	0	/	/
Galveston Co.	1,028	1	0	0	0	~	~	~	~	~
Harris Co.[a,b]	10,891	12	1	/	/	9,657	19	0	/	/
Hood Co.[b]	161	1	0	0	0	~	~	~	~	~
Nueces Co.	950	3	0	0	0	~	~	~	~	~
Travis Co.	2,431	4	1	5	3	2,623	6	1	9	1
Utah										
Beaver Co.[b]	370	1	0	/	/	~	~	~	~	~
Davis Co.	~	~	~	~	~	736	2	1	1	1
Salt Lake Co.	2,125	6	1	23	2	1,880	7	1	0	0
Utah Co.	646	1	0	1	1	685	1	0	1	1
Weber Co. Corr. Fac.	973	1	1	4	2	770	0	0	13	4
Virginia										
Albemarle-Charlottesville Reg. Jail[b]	520	1	0	/	/	538	0	0	0	0
Arlington Co.	~	~	~	~	~	623	0	0	2	1
Blue Ridge Reg. Jail Authority	1,267	1	0	0	0	~	~	~	~	~
Chesapeake City	1,133	0	0	0	0	1,109	0	0	1	0
Fairfax Co. Adult Det. Ctr.	1,325	2	0	1	0	1,311	1	0	1	1
Hampton Roads Reg. Jail	1,233	5	0	0	0	1,240	0	0	0	0
Henrico Co.	1,214	1	0	0	0	1,135	3	1	1	1
New River Valley Reg. Jail[a]	~	~	~	~	~	650	4	0	/	/
Norfolk Municipal Jail	1,638	0	0	5	0	1,727	0	0	4	0
Northern Neck Reg. Jail	451	0	0	1	1	~	~	~	~	~
Northwestern Reg. Adult Det. Ctr.[i]	672	2	1	0	0	~	~	~	~	~
Prince William-Manassas Reg Adult Corr. Ctr.[f]	~	~	~	~	~	722	1	0	/	/
Richmond City	1,527	0	0	0	0	1,564	1	0	0	0
Riverside Reg. Jail	1,192	1	0	0	0	1,146	0	0	0	0
Roanoke City[b]	716	2	0	0	0	~	~	~	~	~
Virginia Beach Municipal Corr. Ctr.[a,b]	1,461	1	0	/	/	1,609	1	0	/	/
Washington										
Benton Co.	672	1	0	0	0	~	~	~	~	~
Clark Co.	~	~	~	~	~	769	2	1	1	0
King Co.[a,b]	2,476	7	1	/	/	2,727	8	0	/	/
Kitsap Co. Corr. Ctr.	371	0	0	0	0	435	1	0	0	0
Pierce Co.[j]	1,334	0	0	1	0	1,471	/	/	0	0
Snohomish Co.	1,225	2	0	3	0	1,284	0	0	2	0
Whatcom Co.	428	3	0	0	0	~	~	~	~	~

Allegations of inmate-on-inmate sexual violence reported by local jail authorities, by year and type of violence, 2007-2008

Jurisdiction and facility	2008					2007				
	Average daily population	Reported inmate-on-inmate nonconsensual sexual acts		Reported inmate-on-inmate abusive sexual contacts		Average daily population	Reported inmate-on-inmate nonconsensual sexual acts		Reported inmate-on-inmate abusive sexual contacts	
		Allegations	Substantiated	Allegations	Substantiated		Allegations	Substantiated	Allegations	Substantiated
West Virginia										
Kanawha Co. South Central Reg. Jail[i]	454	2	0	/	/	453	1	0	1	0
Raleigh Co. Southern Reg. Jail[b]	467	0	0	/	/	524	3	0	0	0
Tygart Valley Reg. Jail	356	3	0	1	0	~	~	~	~	~
Wisconsin										
Brown Co.[a]	~	~	~	~	~	770	1	1	/	/
Dane Co.	926	0	0	1	0	~	~	~	~	~
Milwaukee Co. House of Corr.	1,841	1	0	0	0	2,247	0	0	0	0
Ozaukee Co.	~	~	~	~	~	220	2	0	0	0

~Not applicable.

/Not reported.

[a]Allegations of abusive sexual contacts could not be counted separately from allegations of nonconsensual sexual acts in 2007.

[b]Allegations of abusive sexual contacts could not be counted separately from allegations of nonconsensual sexual acts in 2008.

[c]Counts of nonconsensual sexual acts in 2008 are based on substantiated allegations only.

[d]Counts of nonconsensual sexual acts in 2007 are based on completed acts only.

[e]Counts of nonconsensual sexual acts in 2008 are based on completed acts only.

[f]Jurisdiction did not record allegations of abusive sexual contacts in 2007.

[g]Counts of nonconsensual sexual acts in 2007 are based on substantiated allegations only.

[h]Jurisdiction did not record allegations of nonconsensual sexual acts in 2008.

[i]Jurisdiction did not record allegations of abusive sexual contacts in 2008.

[j]Jurisdiction did not record allegations of nonconsensual sexual acts in 2007.

Local jail authorities with no reported allegations of inmate-on-inmate sexual victimization, 2007-2008

Jurisdiction and facility	Average daily population, 2008	Average daily population, 2007	Jurisdiction and facility	Average daily population, 2008	Average daily population, 2007
Alabama			**Colorado**		
Albertville City	~	37	Adams Co. Det. Fac.[a,b]	1,286	1,300
Baldwin Co.	593	628	Bent Co.	~	22
Bibb Co.	76	~	Garfield Co.	130	~
Brighton City[a]	~	5	Jackson Co.	~	1,194
Cullman Co.	~	5,109	Lincoln Co.[b]	120	~
De Kalb Co.[b]	177	~	Logan Co.	~	120
Gardendale City	19	~	**District of Columbia**		
Geneva Co.	58	~	D.C. Dept. of Corr.	1,911	1,949
Lee Co. Det. Ctr.	338	321	**Florida**		
Madison Co. Det. Fac.	~	967	Bradford Co.	125	~
Mobile Co.	53	51	Clay Co.	~	398
Montgomery Co. Det. Fac.[a]	~	688	Columbia Co. Det. Ctr.[b]	295	~
Opp City	5	~	Dixie Co.	~	91
Pickens Co.[a]	~	91	Highlands Co.	459	~
Saraland City	~	4	Indian River Co.	~	544
Shelby Co.[c]	459	~	Jackson Co. Corr. Fac.[a]	~	226
Talledega Co.[b]	286	~	Lafayette Co.	~	32
Alaska			Lake Co.[a]	~	1,033
Kotzebue Reg. Jail	15	~	Lee Co.	2,218	2,199
Petersburg City	~	1	Martin Co.	611	601
Sitka City	~	5	Osceola Co.	1,160	~
Arizona			Santa Rosa Co.	~	520
Apache Co.	122	~	St. Johns Co.	530	~
Mohave Co.	460	525	Sumter Co. Det. Ctr.	249	275
Navajo Co. Det. Ctr.[c]	349	377	**Georgia**		
Pinal Co.[d]	1,229	904	Augusta-Richmond Co.	1,112	1,239
Arkansas			Bibb Co. Law Enforcement Ctr.	~	751
Ashley Co.	40	~	Chattooga Co.	~	58
Benton Co. Det. Fac.[a]	~	493	Cherokee Co.	549	~
Crawford Co.[a]	~	73	Clarke Co.	365	~
Jackson Co. Det. Ctr.[a]	~	35	Clayton Co.	1,751	1,721
Madison Co.	~	2	Clinch Co.	26	~
Mississippi Co. Det. Ctr.	157	~	Coweta Co.[a,b]	341	330
Montgomery Co.	5	~	Dawson Co.	189	~
Pulaski Co. Reg. Jail	1,129	932	Decatur Co. Corr. Inst.[b]	260	~
St. Francis Co.[g]	~	2,796	Dekalb Co.[a,b]	3,015	3,252
Washington Co. Det. Ctr.[b]	549	~	Dodge Co.	68	~
Yell Co.	14	~	Early Co.	~	39
California			Effingham Co. Prison	~	242
Butte Co.	472	~	Evans Co.[a,e,g]	~	18
Humboldt Co.	~	371	Floyd Co. Prison	739	339
Imperial Co.	502	489	Forsyth Co.	313	~
Kings Co.[b]	357	~	Glynn Co. Det. Ctr.	532	~
Lake Co. Hill Road Corr. Fac.	~	260	Gordon City	0	~
Marin Co.	309	290	Gwinnett Co Dept. of Corr.	682	~
Mendocino Co.	~	308	Hall Co. Det. Ctr.[a]	~	624
Merced Co.	769	~	Houston Co.[a]	~	405
Monterey Co.	1,118	1,120	Jackson Co.	146	~
Placer Co.	~	595	Jeff Davis Co.	44	~
San Bernardino Co. West Valley Det. Ctr.	5,500	5,814	Jones Co.	126	~
Santa Barbara Co.	~	950	Lamar Co.	90	~
Sierra Co.	2	~	Lee Co.	72	~
Siskiyou Co.[a]	~	83	Liberty Co. Jail	~	247
Tuolumne Co.[b]	141	~	Lowndes Co.	702	~
Yolo Co.	~	428	Madison Co.	~	69
Yuba Co.	360	~	McDuffie Co.	~	153
			Mitchell Co. Corr. Inst.	~	140
			Monroe Co.	~	134

Local jail authorities with no reported allegations of inmate-on-inmate sexual victimization, 2007-2008

Jurisdiction and facility	Average daily population, 2008	Average daily population, 2007	Jurisdiction and facility	Average daily population, 2008	Average daily population, 2007
Georgia (continued)			**Kansas**		
Muscogee Co. Prison[a,c]	568	565	Allen Co.	~	53
Newton Co.	626	~	Ford Co.	91	~
Pike Co.	~	3	Johnson Co.[b]	715	863
Spalding Co.	~	459	Lane Co.[b,c]	2	~
Spalding Co. Corr. Inst.[a]	~	378	Linn Co.	8	~
Thomas Co.[a]	~	210	Montgomery Co.	~	144
Troup Co.	465	~	Pratt Co.	~	15
Troup Co. Corr. Inst.	~	351	Smith Co.	7	~
Idaho			**Kentucky**		
Bonneville Co.	238	288	Boone Co.[b]	448	~
Idaho Co.[b]	10	~	Boyd Co.	~	227
Power Co.	~	10	Breckinridge Co.	191	~
Illinois			Casey Co./State Jail	308	~
Adams Co.	~	101	Christian Co.[b]	632	686
De Kalb Co.	~	102	Clay Co. Det. Ctr.	235	~
Du Page Co.[b]	841	820	Crittenden Co.	~	12
Edgar Co.[e,g]	~	4	Graves Co.	~	101
Kankakee Co.	~	506	Grayson Co. Jail & Annex	580	~
Lawrence Co.	~	19	Hardin Co. Det. Ctr.[a]	~	545
McDonough Co.[b]	34	~	Laurel Co.	~	292
Macon Co.	251	~	Pike Co.	300	~
Monroe Co.	10	~	Three Forks Reg. Jail	205	~
Peoria Co.	499	445	Webster Co.	109	108
Rock Island Co.[a]	~	266	**Louisiana**		
Saline Co. Law Enforcement & Det. Ctr.	81	~	Ascension Parish Jail	258	~
Sangamon Co.	340	~	Bayou Dorcheat Corr. Ctr.	~	524
Stephenson Co.[b]	134	~	Beauregard Parish Jail[a]	~	168
Vermilion Co.	~	260	Caddo Parish Corr. Ctr.	1,400	1,450
Indiana			Calvasieu Parish Corr. Ctr.[a,b]	1,249	1,197
Adams Co.	65	~	Caldwell Parish Jails - (3 Facilities)[a,b]	318	318
Allen Co.	~	700	Catahoula Parish Jail & Det. Fac[a]	~	22
Bartholomew Co.[a]	154	192	Claiborne Det. Ctr.	525	~
Delaware Co. Justice Ctr.[a]	318	317	De Soto Parish Jail[c]	110	~
Grant Co. Security Complex	251	~	East Carroll Det. Ctr.	688	1,125
Greene Co.	~	64	Evangeline Parish Jail[d,h]	~	72
Hancock Co.	~	148	Iberia Parish Jail[b]	485	~
Harrison Co.[b]	170	~	La Salle Parish Jail	~	23
Howard Co.	341	~	Morehouse Parish Jail[a,e]	160	535
Jay Co.	~	40	Morgan City	59	~
Johnson Co.	~	290	Ouachita Parish Corr. Fac.	900	~
Knox Co.	~	153	Pointe Coupee Parish Det. Ctr.	174	~
Marion Co.[d]	~	1,361	Rapides Parish	272	~
Porter Co.[a,b]	467	467	St. Charles Parish Jail[b]	532	~
Wells Co.	91	93	St. Tammany Parish	~	746
Iowa			Union Parish Det. Ctr.	360	347
Black Hawk Co.	183	257	West Baton Rouge Parish	~	250
Buena Vista Co.	24	~	**Maine**		
Carroll Co.	~	12	Hancock Co.	44	~
Clinton Co.	9	~	Two Bridges Reg. Jail[a]	~	9,464
Decatur Co.	5	~	**Maryland**		
Delaware Co.	~	7	Carroll Co. Det. Ctr.	271	283
Emmet Co.	8	~	Charles Co. Det. Ctr.	377	~
Howard Co.	~	7	Harford Co. Det. Ctr.	461	400
Marshall Co.	~	146	Prince Georges Co. Corr. Ctr.	1,385	1,486
Polk Co.	648	~	Wicomico Co. Det. Ctr.[a]	492	628
Scott Co. Jail & Annex	8,829	295	Worcester Co.	253	~
Sioux Co.	~	37			

Local jail authorities with no reported allegations of inmate-on-inmate sexual victimization, 2007-2008

Jurisdiction and facility	Average daily population, 2008	Average daily population, 2007	Jurisdiction and facility	Average daily population, 2008	Average daily population, 2007
Massachusetts			**Missouri (continued)**		
Plymouth Co. House of Corr. & Jail[a]	1,516	1,596	St. Clair Co.	~	118
Michigan			St. Louis City[b]	1,672	1,200
Antrim Co.	40	~	Stoddard Co.	65	~
Bay Co. Law Enforcement Ctr.	~	219	**Montana**		
Benzie Co.	~	31	Fallon Co.[a]	~	1
Calhoun Co.	497	~	Flathead Co. Det. Ctr.[d]	~	92
Cass Co.	~	126	Gallatin Co. Det. Ctr.	81	~
Emmet Co.	86	~	Pondera Co.	6	~
Ingham Co.[b,f]	672	685	Sanders Co.	~	20
Kalamazoo Co.[b]	324	365	**Nebraska**		
Mecosta Co.[a]	~	86	Box Butte Co.[b]	16	~
Monroe Co.	328	~	Hamilton Co.	~	6
Saginaw Co.[a]	~	516	Harlan Co.	~	3
St. Clair Co.	428	408	Morrill Co.	~	13
Minnesota			Sarpy Co.	~	153
Anoka Co.	228	~	Thayer Co.	3	~
Beltrami Co.	~	121	**Nevada**		
Dakota Co.	~	335	Las Vegas City Det. Ctr.[b]	820	100
Hennepin Co. Adult Det. Ctr.	728	~	**New Hampshire**		
Hennepin Co. Workhouse	~	582	Carroll Co. House of Corr. & Jail	~	88
Itasca Co.[b]	83	~	Rockingham Co. Jail & House of Corr.	332	~
Koochiching Co. Law Enforcement Ctr.[b]	14	~	**New Jersey**		
Lyon Co. Law Enforcement Ctr.	~	30	Bergen Co. Jail & Annex	~	970
Marshall Co. Law Enforcement Ctr.	~	10	Burlington Co.	~	703
Olmsted Co.	~	280	Gloucester Co.	373	~
Otter Tail Co. Det. Ctr.	58	~	Hunterdon Co.[b]	102	~
Ramsey Co. Corr. Fac.	398	~	Morris Co. Corr. Fac.	327	308
Sherburne Co.[b]	566	581	Somerset Co. Jail & Annex	~	324
Mississippi			**New Mexico**		
Calhoun Co.	~	47	Catron Co.	~	4
Carroll/Montgomery Region Corr. Ctr.	337	~	Curry Co.	37	~
Clarke Co.[b]	44	~	Dona Ana Co. Det. Ctr.	852	~
Clay Co.[e]	~	10	Lea Co.	~	299
Hinds Co.[a,b]	1,042	931	Luna Co.	~	392
Holmes-Humphrey Reg. Corr. Fac.	379	~	Gallup-McKinley Adult Det. Ctr.	328	~
Jackson Co.[b]	412	~	Roosevelt Co.[i]	79	~
Jefferson/Franklin Corr. Fac.	296	~	Sandoval Co.	396	~
Lafayette Co.[a]	~	130	San Juan Co. Det. Ctr.	~	606
Lauderdale Co.[a]	~	270	**New York**		
Leake Co. Corr. Fac.	361	373	Chenango Co.[b]	79	~
Leflore Co.	125	~	Jefferson Co.	142	~
Rankin Co.[a,i]	416	58	Madison Co.	3	~
Walthall Co.	~	22	Monroe Co.[a]	1,343	1,450
Webster Co.	12	~	Montgomery Co.	~	126
Winston/Choctaw Reg. Corr. Fac.[a]	~	350	Nassau Co. Corr. Ctr.[f]	1,607	1,716
Missouri			Niagara Co.[i]	489	~
Arnold Municipal City[a]	~	7	Oneida Co. Corr. Fac.	~	468
Bates Co. Sheriff & Jail[a]	~	104	Onondaga Co. Dept. of Corr.	474	~
Belton City[b]	10	~	Ontario Co.[g]	~	214
Clay Co. Det. Ctr.	322	~	Rensselaer Co.	~	282
Douglas Co.	~	19	Rockland Co. Corr. Ctr.	~	262
Jackson Co. Det. Ctr.[g]	~	784	St. Lawrence Co.	~	112
Kansas City Corr. Inst.	148	~	Suffolk Co.	1,695	1,752
Lincoln Co.[a]	~	147	Tioga Co.	~	83
Marion Co.	6	~	Westchester Co.	1,478	1,465
Montgomery Co.	~	76			
Ozark Co.	16	~			
Pulaski Co.	~	30			
St. Charles Co.	~	329			

Local jail authorities with no reported allegations of inmate-on-inmate sexual victimization, 2007-2008

Jurisdiction and facility	Average daily population, 2008	Average daily population, 2007	Jurisdiction and facility	Average daily population, 2008	Average daily population, 2007
North Carolina			**Pennsylvania**		
Buncombe Co.	409	475	Adams Co.	~	312
Cabarrus Co.	~	217	Blair Co. Prison[i]	304	~
Duplin Co.	~	16	Centre Co. Prison	~	212
Durham Co.[a]	~	618	Clearfield Co. Prison	135	~
Edgecombe Co.[b,h]	282	260	Clinton Co. Prison[b]	318	298
Forsyth Co.	891	~	Erie Co.	632	~
Guilford Co.	~	926	Greene Co. Prison	~	105
Lee Co.[a]	~	161	Lackawanna Co. Prison[a]	1,013	1,072
McDowell Co.[b]	104	~	Lebanon Co. Corr. Fac.[a,b]	518	538
Moore Co[j]	129	~	Lycoming Co. Prison	~	336
Pamlico Co.	~	87	Monroe Co. Corr. Fac.	344	~
Richmond Co.[b]	86	87	Washington Co.[b]	413	~
Robeson Co.[b]	377	~	**South Carolina**		
Rowan Co.	274	~	Abbeville Co. Det. Ctr.[b]	61	~
Vance Co.	~	153	Aiken Co. Det. Ctr.	422	~
Wake Co.	1,331	1,211	Anderson Co.	428	~
Wilson Co.	220	~	Beaufort Co. Det. Ctr.[b]	300	~
North Dakota			Berkeley Co. Det. Ctr.	~	362
Cass Co.	198	175	Dillon Co. Det. Ctr.	~	160
Pembina Co.	7	~	Dorchester Co.	295	~
Ohio			Fairfield Co. Det. Ctr.	6	~
Clermont Co.	304	~	Florence Co. Det. Ctr.	~	426
Clinton Co.	19	~	Greenville Co. Det. Ctr.[a]	1,367	1,418
Crawford Co.	111	112	Horry Co. Det. Ctr.[b]	656	~
Delaware Co.[b]	163	~	Orangeburg-Calhoun Reg. Det. Ctr.	~	336
Fayette Co.[b]	52	~	Pickens Co.	~	96
Greene Co.	~	381	Richland Co. Det. Ctr.	1,153	1,100
Highland Co.	~	71	Spartanburg Co. Det. Fac.[a]	~	919
Lake Co. Adult Det. Ctr.	318	~	York Co. Moss Justice Ctr.[b]	425	~
Mahoning Co.	561	527	**South Dakota**		
Miami Co.[a]	~	104	Bon Homme Co.	~	6
Niles City	2	~	Hughes Co.	48	~
Noble Co.	~	20	Meade Co.	~	45
Richland Co.	~	152	Pennington Co. Jail	420	~
Summit Co. Jail & Glenwood Annex	658	~	Winner City[a,g]	~	63
Oklahoma			**Tennessee**		
Carter Co.	~	185	Carroll Co.[b]	76	74
Comanche Co.[a]	291	298	Greene Co.	366	~
Grady Co.	334	~	Knox Co.	979	~
Latimer Co.	100	~	Lawrence Co.	130	~
Midwest City	~	48	Lincoln Co.[f]	125	~
Muldrow City	~	6	Loudon Co.[b,f]	91	~
Muskogee Co./City Det. Ctr.	~	287	Madison Co. Penal Farm	~	80
Roger Mills Co.[h]	~	17	Marion Co.	~	101
Rogers Co.[b]	192	~	Monroe Co.	~	165
Stephens Co.[a]	~	108	Putnam Co.	~	208
Washington Co.	102	91	Sequatchie Co.	~	90
Woodward Co.[b,c]	31	~	Sevier Co.[b]	366	305
Oregon			Sullivan Co.	675	584
Clackamas Co.[a]	~	336	Sumner Co.[a]	~	616
Grant Co.	24	~	Warren Co.[b]	212	~
Lake Co.	~	15	Washington Co.[i,j]	519	~
Lane Co.	330	558	Williamson Co.[a,b]	311	341
Polk Co.	~	115	Wilson Co.	~	250
Tillamook Co.[b]	73	~			

Local jail authorities with no reported allegations of inmate-on-inmate sexual victimization, 2007-2008

Jurisdiction and facility	Average daily population, 2008	Average daily population, 2007	Jurisdiction and facility	Average daily population, 2008	Average daily population, 2007
Texas			**Virginia (continued)**		
Angelina Co.	258	~	Rappahannock Co.	~	16
Bandera Co. Law Enforcement Ctr.	~	12	Rappahannock Reg. Jail & Annex[b]	1,017	1,003
Bell Co. Law Enforcement Ctr.	672	~	Roanoke Co.	286	~
Bowie Co.	~	895	Rockingham Reg. Jail	~	295
Brazos Co.[c,f]	553	~	Southwest Virginia Reg.	1,102	1,379
Burnet Co.	~	89	Virginia Peninsula Reg. Jail	~	489
Caldwell Co.[g]	~	168	**Washington**		
Cameron Co.[a]	100	971	Asotin Co.[a]	~	47
Chambers Co.[g]	~	114	Buckley City[b]	22	~
Denton Co. Det. Ctr.[a]	1,121	1,065	Kent City[d]	~	139
Edwards Co.	9	~	Kirkland City	~	7
Fayette Co. Justice Ctr.	21	37	Skagit Co.	237	~
Grayson Co.	~	382	Spokane Co. Geiger Corr. Ctr.	510	562
Guadalupe Co. Det. Ctr.[a]	378	460	**West Virginia**		
Harrison Co.	133	~	Marshall Co. Northern Reg Jail & Corr. Complex	~	314
Hays Co.	315	~	North Central Reg. Jail	517	~
Hidalgo Co. Adult Det. Ctr.[b,g]	1,132	1,185	Western Reg. Jail[e,g]	~	461
Hunt Co. Criminal Justice Ctr.[b,f]	384	~	**Wisconsin**		
Jasper Co. Law Enforcement Ctr.[a]	~	62	Adams Co.	~	64
Jefferson Co. Det. Ctr.[a,b]	924	1,176	Barron Co. Justice Ctr.	~	123
Lipscomb Co.	~	2	Burnett Co. Law Enforcement Ctr.[b]	30	~
Lubbock Co.[a]	724	1,000	Dodge Co.	462	463
McLennan Co.	869	860	Dunn Co.[c]	113	~
Maverick Co.	~	230	Eau Claire Co.	~	274
Midland Co.	~	280	Marathon Co. Adult Det. Fac.[d]	~	300
Mills Co.	7	~	Milwaukee Co.	890	947
Montgomery Co.	815	1,112	Racine Co.[b]	788	~
Parker Co.[b]	310	~	Richland Co.[a]	~	27
Randall Co.	~	272	Rock Co.	~	521
Rusk Co.[a,b]	89	88	Shawano Co.	510	~
San Patricio Co.	192	~	Waukesha Co.	655	~
Shelby Co.	~	51	Winnebago Co.	319	~
Sherman Co.	~	2	**Wyoming**		
Tarrant Co.[a,b]	3,333	3,377	Fremont Co.	~	166
Tom Green Co.[a]	~	415	Laramie Co.	222	~
Upton Co.	38	~	Natrona Co. Det. Ctr.[a]	~	297
Victoria Co.[b]	450	~	Platte Co.	97	~
Walker Co.	~	130	Sheridan Co.	90	~
Wichita Co.[i]	435	435	Sweetwater Co.[a]	~	119
Zavala Co.	9	~			
Utah					
Cache Co.[a]	~	306			
Tooele Co.	~	119			
Virginia					
Accomack Co.	~	113			
Alexandria City Det. Ctr.[b]	540	~			
Botetourt Co.[b]	91	~			
Central Virginia Reg. Jail	372	395			
Danville City	~	208			
Danville City Prison Farm[a,b,c,e,f,g]	149	164			
Middle River Reg. Jail	651	~			
Newport News City	629	~			
Pamunkey Reg. Jail	~	455			
Patrick Co.	27	~			
Peumansend Creek Reg. Jail[a]	275	288			

~Not applicable. Facility not sampled in survey year.

[a]Allegations of abusive sexual contacts could not be counted separately from allegations of nonconsensual sexual acts in 2007.

[b]Allegations of abusive sexual contacts could not be counted separately from allegations of nonconsensual sexual acts in 2008.

[c]Counts of nonconsensual sexual acts in 2008 are based on substantiated allegations only.

[d]Jurisdiction did not record allegations of abusive sexual contacts in 2007.

[e]Counts of nonconsensual sexual acts in 2007 are based on completed acts only.

[f]Counts of nonconsensual sexual acts in 2008 are based on completed acts only.

[g]Counts of nonconsensual sexual acts in 2007 are based on substantiated allegations only.

[h]Jurisdiction did not record allegations of nonconsensual sexual acts in 2007.

[i]Jurisdiction did not record allegations of abusive sexual contacts in 2008.

[j]Jurisdiction did not record allegations of nonconsensual sexual acts in 2008.

Allegations of staff-on-inmate sexual victimization reported by local jail authorities, by year and type of victimization, 2007-2008

	2008					2007				
	Average daily population	Reported staff-on-inmate sexual misconduct		Reported staff-on-inmate sexual harassment		Average daily population	Reported staff-on-inmate sexual misconduct		Reported staff-on-inmate sexual harassment	
Jurisdiction and facility		Allegations	Substantiated	Allegations	Substantiated		Allegations	Substantiated	Allegations	Substantiated
Total	/	239	38	87	9	/	256	73	79	15
Alabama										
Calhoun Co.[a,b]	343	0	0	/	/	400	1	1	/	/
Cullman Co.[c]	~	~	~	~	~	5,109	1	1	0	0
Jefferson Co.[a,b]	1,099	0	0	/	/	1,212	2	0	/	/
Lee Co. Det. Ctr.	338	0	0	0	0	321	1	1	0	0
Morgan Co. & Annex	~	~	~	~	~	270	1	1	0	0
Arizona										
Maricopa Co.[a,b]	9,249	3	2	/	/	9,241	0	0	/	/
Pima Co. Adult Det. Ctr.	1,921	1	0	1	1	1,891	1	0	0	0
Pinal Co.	1,229	1	1	0	0	904	0	0	0	0
Arkansas										
Faulkner Co. Det. Ctr.	373	1	0	0	0	325	0	0	0	0
Pulaski Co. Reg. Jail	1,129	1	1	0	0	932	0	0	0	0
California										
Contra Costa Co.	1,612	0	0	0	0	1,600	1	1	0	0
Fresno Co.	2,961	2	2	1	0	2,861	0	0	0	0
Humboldt Co.[a]	~	~	~	~	~	371	1	0	/	/
Imperial Co.	502	0	0	0	0	489	3	1	0	0
Kern Co.	2,260	1	0	0	0	2,392	0	0	0	0
Los Angeles Co.-Custody Support Svs.[b]	19,569	1	0	/	/	19,374	2	1	0	0
Riverside Co.	3,481	1	0	0	0	3,521	1	1	0	0
San Bernardino Co. West Valley Det. Ctr.	5,500	4	2	0	0	5,814	0	0	0	0
San Diego Co.	5,184	4	0	0	0	5,072	0	0	1	0
San Francisco City & Co.	2,086	2	0	0	0	2,011	0	0	1	0
San Joaquin Co.[a,b]	1,500	2	1	/	/	1,566	0	0	/	/
Santa Clara Co.[a]	4,610	3	2	0	0	4,640	0	0	/	/
Colorado										
Arapahoe Co.	1,171	0	0	0	0	1,352	0	0	1	0
Bent Co.[a]	~	~	~	~	~	22	2	1	/	/
El Paso Co.	1,538	0	0	0	0	1,522	1	0	0	0
Jefferson Co.	1,182	0	0	2	0	1,302	0	0	0	0
Larimer Co. Det. Ctr.	463	1	0	0	0	537	0	0	1	0
Weld Co.	690	2	1	0	0	~	~	~	~	~
District of Columbia										
D.C. Dept. of Corr.	1,911	0	0	0	0	1,949	4	0	1	0
Florida										
Alachua Co.[a,b]	910	1	0	/	/	1,079	1	1	/	/
Brevard Co. Det. Ctr.	1,812	1	0	0	0	1,797	0	0	0	0
Broward Co.	5,364	6	0	6	0	5,305	5	1	2	0
Collier Co.	1,138	4	1	0	0	1,224	1	1	0	0
Highlands Co.	459	1	0	0	0	~	~	~	~	~
Lee Co.	2,218	0	0	0	0	2,199	1	0	0	0
Manatee Co.	1,294	0	0	0	0	1,423	2	0	0	0
Marion Co.	1,832	0	0	0	0	2,007	1	0	0	0
Miami-Dade Co. Corr. & Rehab.	7,013	6	0	4	1	6,975	0	0	4	0
Palm Beach Co.	2,980	0	0	0	0	2,555	1	1	0	0
Polk Co.	2,374	1	1	0	0	2,466	2	2	2	2
Volusia Co.	1,383	1	0	0	0	1,533	0	0	0	0
Georgia										
Cherokee Co.	549	1	0	0	0	~	~	~	~	~
Clayton Co.	1,751	0	0	0	0	1,721	1	1	3	3
Fulton Co.[a,b]	2,846	0	0	/	/	2,834	1	0	/	/
Gwinnett Co.	2,691	1	0	1	0	2,478	2	0	0	0

Allegations of staff-on-inmate sexual victimization reported by local jail authorities, by year and type of victimization, 2007-2008

| Jurisdiction and facility | 2008 | | | | | 2007 | | | | |
| | Average daily population | Reported staff-on-inmate sexual misconduct | | Reported staff-on-inmate sexual harassment | | Average daily population | Reported staff-on-inmate sexual misconduct | | Reported staff-on-inmate sexual harassment | |
		Allegations	Substantiated	Allegations	Substantiated		Allegations	Substantiated	Allegations	Substantiated
Georgia (continued)										
Muscogee Co.	565	3	0	1	1	~	~	~	~	~
Spalding Co.	~	~	~	~	~	459	1	0	0	0
Walton Co.	419	0	0	0	0	371	1	1	0	0
Idaho										
Ada Co.	980	0	0	0	0	920	0	0	2	0
Illinois										
Cook Co. - Dept. of Corr.	9,355	2	1	0	0	9,600	1	1	0	0
Du Page Co.	841	1	0	0	0	820	0	0	0	0
Edgar Co.	~	~	~	~	~	4	1	0	0	0
Peoria Co.	499	0	0	0	0	445	1	0	0	0
Winnebago Co.[e]	758	1	0	0	0	665	0	0	0	0
Indiana										
Porter Co.[a,b]	467	1	1	/	/	467	0	0	/	/
Vigo Co.	290	2	1	0	0	~	~	~	~	~
Wells Co.	91	1	0	0	0	93	0	0	0	0
Iowa										
Polk Co.	648	0	0	2	0	~	~	~	~	~
Kansas										
Allen Co.	~	~	~	~	~	53	2	2	0	0
Sedgwick Co.	1,553	0	0	1	0	1,522	4	1	0	0
Shawnee Co. Adult Det. Division	~	~	~	~	~	475	2	0	1	1
Kentucky										
Daviess Co. Det. Ctr.	~	~	~	~	~	614	1	0	0	0
Franklin Co. Reg. Jail	~	~	~	~	~	319	2	0	0	0
Henderson Co. Det. Ctr.[d,e]	547	2	1	/	/	496	0	0	2	0
Lexington-Fayette Co. Det. Div.[d]	1,237	5	0	/	/	1,252	3	3	0	0
Louisville Metropolitan Dept. of Corr.[b]	1,902	3	1	/	/	1,810	1	1	4	0
Louisiana										
Beauregard Parish Jail	~	~	~	~	~	168	2	2	0	0
Caddo Parish Corr. Ctr.	1,400	0	0	0	0	1,450	3	0	0	0
Claiborne Det. Ctr.	525	3	1	0	0	~	~	~	~	~
Lafayette Parish Jail	~	~	~	~	~	1,090	1	1	1	1
West Baton Rouge Parish	~	~	~	~	~	250	1	0	0	0
Maine										
Cumberland Co.	402	1	0	0	0	462	1	0	0	0
Two Bridges Reg. Jail	~	~	~	~	~	9,464	1	1	0	0
Maryland										
Anne Arundel Co.[a]	1,128	0	0	0	0	1,123	4	0	/	/
Baltimore Co. Bureau of Corr.	1,360	0	0	1	0	1,356	0	0	0	0
Caroline Co.	~	~	~	~	~	100	1	0	0	0
Carroll Co. Det. Ctr.	271	0	0	0	0	283	3	0	0	0
Montgomery Co.	~	~	~	~	~	998	2	1	1	0
Wicomico Co. Det. Ctr.[a]	492	1	1	0	0	628	1	0	/	/
Massachusetts										
Barnstable Co. Jail & House of Corr.	416	1	0	0	0	440	0	0	2	0
Bristol Co.	1,483	4	0	1	0	1,472	1	0	0	0
Essex Co. Corr. Fac.	1,624	2	0	0	0	1,631	0	0	0	0
Hampden Co.	1,911	0	0	0	0	2,138	1	0	1	0
Middlesex Co. Jail & House of Corr.	1,294	0	0	0	0	1,326	1	0	1	0
Suffolk Co.	711	1	0	0	0	698	0	0	0	0
Suffolk Co. House of Corr.	1,733	1	1	0	0	1,685	1	0	0	0
Worcester Co. Jail & House of Corr.[b]	1,282	1	0	/	/	1,415	0	0	0	0

Allegations of staff-on-inmate sexual victimization reported by local jail authorities, by year and type of victimization, 2007-2008

| | 2008 | | | | | 2007 | | | | |
| | Average daily population | Reported staff-on-inmate sexual misconduct | | Reported staff-on-inmate sexual harassment | | Average daily population | Reported staff-on-inmate sexual misconduct | | Reported staff-on-inmate sexual harassment | |
Jurisdiction and facility		Allegations	Substantiated	Allegations	Substantiated		Allegations	Substantiated	Allegations	Substantiated
Michigan										
Berrien Co.	363	1	0	0	0	388	0	0	0	0
Macomb Co.	1,361	0	0	0	0	1,398	1	1	0	0
Oakland Co.	1,814	1	0	0	0	1,961	0	0	0	0
Minnesota										
Sherburne Co.[b,c]	566	0	0	/	/	581	1	0	1	0
Mississippi										
Missouri										
Bates Co. Sheriff & Jail	~	~	~	~	~	104	1	0	0	0
Kansas City Corr. Inst.	148	8	0	0	0	~	~	~	~	~
Pulaski Co.	~	~	~	~	~	30	1	0	0	0
St. Clair Co.	~	~	~	~	~	118	1	1	0	0
St. Louis City	1,672	1	0	18	0	1,200	0	0	0	0
St. Louis Co. - Dept. of Justice Services	1,186	2	1	0	0	~	~	~	~	~
Montana										
Gallatin Co. Det. Ctr.	81	5	0	0	0	~	~	~	~	~
Nebraska										
Sarpy Co.	~	~	~	~	~	153	1	0	0	0
Nevada										
Clark Co. Det. Ctr.	3,061	3	0	0	0	3,745	4	0	0	0
Washoe Co. Det. Ctr.	1,048	3	0	0	0	1,200	0	0	0	0
Las Vegas City Det. Ctr.	820	0	0	0	0	100	1	0	0	0
New Hampshire										
Carroll Co. House of Corr. & Jail	~	~	~	~	~	88	0	0	2	0
Strafford Co.	~	~	~	~	~	405	1	1	0	0
New Jersey										
Atlantic Co. Jail - Dept. of Public Safety[a]	914	1	0	0	0	909	2	0	/	/
Essex Co. Corr. Fac.	2,332	1	0	0	0	3,028	0	0	0	0
Hudson Co. Corr. Fac.	1,885	1	0	0	0	1,946	1	0	0	0
Hunterdon Co.[b]	102	1	0	/	/	~	~	~	~	~
Mercer Co. Corr. Ctr.[b]	995	3	3	/	/	~	~	~	~	~
Middlesex Co. Adult Corr. Ctr.[a]	1,204	1	0	0	0	980	0	0	/	/
Monmouth Co. Corr. Inst.	977	1	0	1	0	1,209	0	0	0	0
Morris Co. Corr. Fac.	327	1	0	0	0	308	0	0	0	0
Passaic Co.[a]	1,509	1	0	0	0	1,912	0	0	/	/
Union Co.	8,085	0	0	1	0	1,070	0	0	0	0
New Mexico										
Bernalillo Co./City Det. Ctr.	5,483	1	0	0	0	2,613	5	3	0	0
Gallup-Mckinley Adult Det. Ctr.	328	3	0	0	0	~	~	~	~	~
New York										
Nassau Co. Corr. Ctr.	1,607	1	0	0	0	1,716	2	0	1	0
New York City	13,546	28	0	11	0	14,064	18	0	10	0
Ontario Co.[c]	~	~	~	~	~	214	1	0	0	0
Rensselaer Co.	~	~	~	~	~	282	1	0	0	0
Suffolk Co.	1,695	1	0	1	0	1,752	0	0	0	0
Westchester Co.	1,478	2	0	0	0	1,465	1	0	0	0
North Carolina										
Durham Co.[a]	~	~	~	~	~	618	1	0	/	/
Mecklenburg Co.[b]	2,578	1	0	/	/	2,585	4	0	2	1
North Dakota										
Cass Co.	198	0	0	0	0	175	2	0	0	0

Allegations of staff-on-inmate sexual victimization reported by local jail authorities, by year and type of victimization, 2007-2008

	2008					2007				
	Average daily population	Reported staff-on-inmate sexual misconduct		Reported staff-on-inmate sexual harassment		Average daily population	Reported staff-on-inmate sexual misconduct		Reported staff-on-inmate sexual harassment	
Jurisdiction and facility		Allegations	Substantiated	Allegations	Substantiated		Allegations	Substantiated	Allegations	Substantiated
Ohio										
Cuyahoga Co. Corr. Ctr.	1,941	0	0	2	1	1,978	1	0	0	0
Franklin Co.[a]	2,202	0	0	1	1	2,314	0	0	/	/
Highland Co.	~	~	~	~	~	71	1	0	6	0
Lake Co. Adult Det. Ctr.	318	1	1	0	0	~	~	~	~	~
Oregon										
Clackamas Co.	~	~	~	~	~	336	1	0	0	0
Deschutes Co. Corr. Fac.	201	0	0	0	0	210	1	0	0	0
Lane Co.	330	2	0	0	0	558	2	0	1	0
Multnomah Co. Det. Fac.	1,502	12	1	4	1	1,592	14	0	5	1
Pennsylvania										
Clinton Co. Prison[b]	318	0	0	/	/	298	1	0	0	0
Dauphin Co. Prison	~	~	~	~	~	979	2	0	0	0
Franklin Co. Prison	358	0	0	2	0	343	0	0	0	0
Lackawanna Co. Prison	1,013	0	0	0	0	1,072	1	0	0	0
Lancaster Co. Prison	1,160	0	0	0	0	1,197	3	1	0	0
Montgomery Co Prison Corr. Fac.	1,742	0	0	0	0	1,614	1	0	0	0
Northampton Co. Dept. of Corr.	779	0	0	1	1	906	0	0	0	0
Philadelphia Prison System[b]	9,287	2	0	/	/	10,200	21	12	0	0
South Carolina										
Dillon Co. Det. Ctr.	~	~	~	~	~	160	1	1	0	0
Dorchester Co.	295	1	1	0	0	~	~	~	~	~
Orangeburg-Calhoun Reg. Det. Ctr.	~	~	~	~	~	336	1	0	1	0
Richland Co. Det. Ctr.	1,153	0	0	0	0	1,100	0	0	6	0
Spartanburg Co. Det. Fac.	~	~	~	~	~	919	0	0	1	1
York Co Moss Justice Ctr.[b]	425	1	0	/	/	~	~	~	~	~
Davidson Co. Sheriffs Office	2,470	3	2	0	0	2,470	9	7	1	1
Knox Co.	979	2	0	2	0	~	~	~	~	~
Sequatchie Co.	~	~	~	~	~	90	2	0	0	0
Sevier Co.	366	1	0	1	0	305	0	0	0	0
Shelby Co. Justice Ctr.	2,678	2	1	1	0	2,733	1	0	1	0
Texas										
Bexar Co. Adult Det. Ctr.[a]	4,211	4	0	0	0	3,176	3	0	/	/
Burnet Co.	~	~	~	~	~	89	1	0	0	0
Chambers Co.	~	~	~	~	~	114	1	0	0	0
Dallas Co.	6,157	0	0	0	0	7,180	1	0	0	0
Grayson Co.[a]	~	~	~	~	~	382	1	0	/	/
Harris Co.	10,891	6	1	1	1	9,657	3	0	0	0
Hunt Co. Criminal Justice Ctr.[b]	384	2	0	/	/	~	~	~	~	~
Travis Co.	2,431	1	0	0	0	2,623	4	0	1	0
Utah										
Davis Co.	~	~	~	~	~	736	1	1	0	0
Salt Lake Co.	2,125	1	0	7	0	1,880	9	7	2	2
Utah Co.[b]	646	1	1	/	/	685	0	0	0	0
Virginia										
Arlington Co.	~	~	~	~	~	623	2	0	0	0
Blue Ridge Reg. Jail Authority	1,267	2	0	0	0	~	~	~	~	~
Chesapeake City	1,133	3	1	2	0	1,109	2	0	1	1
Fairfax Co. Adult Det. Ctr.	1,325	0	0	0	0	1,311	1	0	0	0
Hampton Roads Reg. Jail	1,233	2	0	0	0	1,240	0	0	0	0
Henrico Co.	1,214	0	0	0	0	1,135	1	1	0	0
New River Valley Reg. Jail	~	~	~	~	~	650	4	0	0	0
Northwestern Reg. Adult Det. Ctr.	672	3	0	0	0	~	~	~	~	~

Allegations of staff-on-inmate sexual victimization reported by local jail authorities, by year and type of victimization, 2007-2008

Jurisdiction and facility	2008 Average daily population	Reported staff-on-inmate sexual misconduct		Reported staff-on-inmate sexual harassment		2007 Average daily population	Reported staff-on-inmate sexual misconduct		Reported staff-on-inmate sexual harassment	
		Allegations	Substantiated	Allegations	Substantiated		Allegations	Substantiated	Allegations	Substantiated
Virginia (continued)										
Pamunkey Reg. Jail	~	~	~	~	~	455	1	0	0	0
Prince William-Manassas Reg Adult Corr. Ctr.[a]	~	~	~	~	~	722	2	2	/	/
Richmond City	1,527	0	0	0	0	1,564	1	0	0	0
Riverside Reg. Jail	1,192	1	1	1	0	1,146	3	2	0	0
Roanoke City[b]	716	1	1	/	/	~	~	~	~	~
Southwest Virginia Reg.	1,102	0	0	0	0	1,379	1	1	0	0
Virginia Beach Municipal Corr. Ctr.	1,461	1	0	0	0	1,609	1	0	0	0
Washington										
Clark Co.	~	~	~	~	~	769	5	1	1	1
King Co.	2,476	10	0	7	0	2,727	6	0	1	0
Kitsap Co. Corr. Ctr.	371	0	0	1	0	435	0	0	0	0
Pierce Co.[b]	1,334	4	0	/	/	1,471	3	0	0	0
Snohomish Co.	1,225	3	0	0	0	1,284	0	0	0	0
West Virginia										
Kanawha Co. South Central Reg. Jail[b]	454	2	1	/	/	453	0	0	2	0
Raleigh Co. Southern Reg. Jail[b]	467	1	0	/	/	524	0	0	0	0
Wisconsin										
Dunn Co.	113	1	0	0	0	~	~	~	~	~
Marathon Co. Adult Det. Fac.[a]	~	~	~	~	~	300	1	0	/	/
Milwaukee Co.	890	0	0	0	0	947	1	1	0	0
Milwaukee Co. House of Corr.	1,841	2	0	0	0	2,247	0	0	2	0
Winnebago Co.	319	0	0	1	1	~	~	~	~	~

~Not applicable.

/Not reported.

[a]Allegations of staff sexual harassment could not be counted separately from allegations of staff sexual misconduct in 2007.

[b]Allegations of staff sexual harassment could not be counted separately from allegations of staff sexual misconduct in 2008.

[c]Counts of staff sexual misconduct in 2007 are based on substantiated allegations only.

[d]Jurisdiction did not record allegations of staff sexual harassment in 2008.

[e]Counts of staff sexual misconduct in 2008 are based on substantiated allegations only.

Local jail authorities with no reported allegations of staff-on-inmate sexual victimization, 2007-2008

Jurisdiction and facility	Average daily population, 2008	Average daily population, 2007	Jurisdiction and facility	Average daily population, 2008	Average daily population, 2007
Alabama			Sonoma Co.	1,027	1,056
Albertville City	~	37	Stanislaus Co.	1,339	1,368
Baldwin Co.	593	628	Tulare Co.	1,529	1,527
Bibb Co.	76	~	Tuolumne Co.	141	~
Brighton City[a]	~	5	Ventura Co.	835	850
De Kalb Co.[b]	177	~	Yolo Co.	~	428
Etowah Co. Det. Ctr.	812	~	Yuba Co.	360	~
Gardendale City	19	~	**Colorado**		
Geneva Co.	58	~	Adams Co. Det. Fac.	1,286	1,300
Madison Co. Det. Fac.	~	967	Denver Co.[a,b]	2,281	2,395
Mobile Co.	53	51	Garfield Co.	130	~
Montgomery Co. Det. Fac.[a]	~	688	Jackson Co.	~	1,194
Opp City	5	~	Lincoln Co.[b]	120	~
Pickens Co.[c]	~	91	Logan Co.	~	120
Saraland City	~	4	Mesa Co. Det. Fac.	347	368
Shelby Co.	459	~	**Florida**		
Talledega Co.	286	~	Bradford Co.	125	~
Alaska			Clay Co.[a]	~	398
Kotzebue Reg. Jail	15	~	Columbia Co. Det. Ctr.[b]	295	~
Petersburg City	~	1	Dixie Co.	~	91
Sitka City	~	5	Escambia Co.	1,812	1,881
Arizona			Hillsborough Co.[a]	3,847	4,015
Apache Co.	122	~	Indian River Co.	~	544
Mohave Co.	460	525	Jackson Co. Corr. Fac.[a]	~	226
Navajo Co. Det. Ctr.	349	377	Jacksonville City	3,727	3,629
Arkansas			Lafayette Co.	~	32
Ashley Co.	40	~	Lake Co.[a]	~	1,033
Benton Co. Det. Fac.[a]	~	493	Leon Co. Det. Fac.[a]	1,132	1,153
Craighead Co. Det. Ctr.	311	~	Martin Co.	611	601
Crawford Co.	~	73	Okeechobee Co.	263	~
Jackson Co. Det. Ctr.	~	35	Orange Co.	4,454	4,096
Madison Co.	~	2	Osceola Co.	1,160	~
Mississippi Co. Det. Ctr.	157	~	Pasco Co.	1,277	1,271
Montgomery Co.	5	~	Pinellas Co.[a]	3,368	3,593
St. Francis Co.	~	2,796	Santa Rosa Co.[a]	~	520
Sebastian Co. Adult Det. Ctr.	~	381	Sarasota Co.	1,019	1,045
Washington Co. Det. Ctr.[b]	549	~	Seminole Co. Corr. Fac.	1,003	~
Yell Co.	14	~	St. Johns Co.[b]	530	~
California			St. Lucie Co. Main Jail	1,550	1,434
Alameda Co.	4,431	4,278	Sumter Co. Det. Ctr.	249	275
Butte Co.	472	~	**Georgia**		
Kings Co.[b]	357	~	Augusta-Richmond Co.	1,112	1,239
Lake Co. Hill Road Corr. Fac.[a]	~	260	Bibb Co. Law Enforcement Ctr.	~	751
Madera Co.	350	~	Carroll Co.	~	533
Marin Co.	309	290	Chatham Co. Adult Det. Ctr.[a,e]	1,739	1,718
Mendocino Co.	~	308	Chattooga Co.[a]	~	58
Merced Co.	769	~	Clarke Co.	365	~
Monterey Co.	1,118	1,120	Clinch Co.[b]	26	~
Orange Co.	6,178	6,360	Cobb Co. Sheriff's Office Jail & Prison Unit[a]	2,490	2,104
Placer Co.	~	595	Coweta Co.[a]	341	330
Sacramento Co.	4,575	2,139	Dawson Co.	189	~
San Mateo Co.[c,d]	1,125	1,198	Decatur Co. Corr. Inst.	260	~
Santa Barbara Co.	~	950	Dekalb Co.	3,015	3,252
Sierra Co.	2	~	Dodge Co.	68	~
Siskiyou Co.	~	83	Dougherty Co.	831	816
Solano Co.[b]	937	1,065	Early Co.	~	39

Local jail authorities with no reported allegations of staff-on-inmate sexual victimization, 2007-2008

Jurisdiction and facility	Average daily population, 2008	Average daily population, 2007	Jurisdiction and facility	Average daily population, 2008	Average daily population, 2007
Effingham Co. Prison	~	242	Grant Co. Security Complex	251	~
Evans Co.[c]	~	18	Greene Co.	~	64
Floyd Co. Prison	739	339	Hamilton Co.	~	327
Forsyth Co.	313	~	Hancock Co.	~	148
Glynn Co. Det. Ctr.	532	~	Harrison Co.	170	~
Gordon City	0	~	Howard Co.[f]	341	~
Gordon Co.	249	~	Jay Co.	~	40
Gwinnett Co Dept. of Corr.	682	~	Johnson Co.	~	290
Hall Co. Det. Ctr.[a]	~	624	Knox Co.	~	153
Houston Co.[a]	~	405	Lake Co.[a,f]	923	937
Jackson Co.[d]	146	~	Marion Co.	~	1,361
Jeff Davis Co.	44	~	St. Joseph Co.	650	~
Jones Co.[f]	126	~	Vanderburgh Co.[c,e]	~	708
Lamar Co.	90	~	**Iowa**		
Lee Co.	72	~	Black Hawk Co.	183	257
Liberty Co. Jail	~	247	Buena Vista Co.	24	~
Lowndes Co.	702	~	Carroll Co.	~	12
Madison Co.	~	69	Clinton Co.	9	~
McDuffie Co.	~	153	Decatur Co.	5	~
Mitchell Co. Corr. Inst.	~	140	Delaware Co.	~	7
Monroe Co.	~	134	Emmet Co.	8	~
Muscogee Co. Prison[a,f]	568	565	Howard Co.	~	7
Newton Co.	626	~	Marshall Co.	~	146
Pike Co.	~	3	Scott Co. Jail & Annex	8,829	295
Spalding Co. Corr. Inst.	~	378	Sioux Co.	~	37
Thomas Co.	~	210	**Kansas**		
Troup Co.	465	~	Chautauqua Co.[a]	~	9
Troup Co. Corr. Inst.	~	351	Ford Co.	91	~
Ware Co.	383	~	Johnson Co.[b]	715	863
Idaho			Lane Co.[b]	2	~
Bonneville Co.	238	288	Linn Co.	8	~
Canyon Co.	479	~	Montgomery Co.	~	144
Idaho Co.[b]	10	~	Pratt Co.	~	15
Kootenai Co.	~	379	Smith Co.	7	~
Power Co.[a]	~	10	**Kentucky**		
Twin Falls Co.	203	~	Boone Co.[b]	448	~
Illinois			Boyd Co.	~	227
Adams Co.	~	101	Breckinridge Co.[b]	191	~
De Kalb Co.	~	102	Campbell Co.[b]	425	427
Kane Co.	671	615	Casey Co./State Jail	308	~
Kankakee Co.[a]	~	506	Christian Co.[b]	632	686
Lawrence Co.	~	19	Clark Co. Det.[a]	~	8
McDonough Co.	34	~	Clay Co. Det. Ctr.	235	~
Macon Co.	251	~	Crittenden Co.	~	12
Monroe Co.	10	~	Graves Co.	~	101
Rock Island Co.	~	266	Grayson Co. Jail & Annex	580	~
Saline Co. Law Enforcement & Det. Ctr.	81	~	Hardin Co. Det. Ctr.[a]	~	545
Sangamon Co.	340	~	Laurel Co.	~	292
Stephenson Co.	134	~	Pike Co.	300	~
Vermilion Co.	~	260	Three Forks Reg. Jail	205	~
Indiana			Webster Co.	109	108
Adams Co.	65	~	**Louisiana**		
Allen Co.	~	700	Ascension Parish Jail	258	~
Bartholomew Co.	154	192	Avoyelles Parish	1,231	1,230
Delaware Co. Justice Ctr.	318	317	Bayou Dorcheat Corr. Ctr.[c]	~	524
Elkhart Co. Security Ctr. (Jail)[b]	747	~	Bossier Parish	1,262	~

Local jail authorities with no reported allegations of staff-on-inmate sexual victimization, 2007-2008

Jurisdiction and facility	Average daily population, 2008	Average daily population, 2007	Jurisdiction and facility	Average daily population, 2008	Average daily population, 2007
Calcasieu Parish Corr. Ctr.[a]	1,249	1,197	Hennepin Co. Workhouse	~	582
Caldwell Parish Jails - (3 Facilities)[a]	318	318	Hennepin Co. Adult Det. Ctr.	728	~
Catahoula Parish Jail & Det. Fac	~	22	Itasca Co.	83	~
De Soto Parish Jail	110	~	Koochiching Co. Law Enforcement Ctr.	14	~
East Baton Rouge Prison[a]	1,671	1,606	Lyon Co. Law Enforcement Ctr.	~	30
East Carroll Det. Ctr.[a]	688	1,125	Marshall Co. Law Enforcement Ctr.	~	10
Evangeline Parish Jail	~	72	Nobles Co.[a]	~	57
Iberia Parish Jail[b]	485	~	Olmsted Co.	~	280
Jefferson Parish Jail	~	839	Otter Tail Co. Det. Ctr.	58	~
La Salle Parish Jail	~	23	Ramsey Co. Corr. Fac.	398	~
Morehouse Parish Jail[a]	160	535	**Mississippi**		
Morgan City	59	~	Calhoun Co.	~	47
New Orleans Parish Prison System	2,570	2,685	Carroll/Montgomery Region Corr. Ctr.	337	~
Ouachita Parish Corr. Fac.	900	~	Clarke Co.[b]	44	~
Pointe Coupee Parish Det. Ctr.	174	~	Clay Co.	~	10
Rapides Parish	272	~	Harrison Co.	1,160	1,150
Richland Parish Det. Ctr.[b]	854	840	Hinds Co.[a]	1,042	931
Sherman Walker Corr. Ctr.	~	298	Holmes-Humphrey Reg. Corr. Fac	379	~
St. Charles Parish Jail	532	~	Jackson Co.[b]	412	~
St. Landry Parish Jail	~	23	Jefferson Franklin Corr. Fac.	296	~
St. Tammany Parish	~	746	Lafayette Co.[a]	~	130
Terrebonne Parish Jail	670	~	Lauderdale Co.	~	270
Union Parish Det. Ctr.	360	347	Leake Co. Corr. Fac.	361	373
Maine			Leflore Co.	125	~
Hancock Co.	44	~	Rankin Co.[a,d]	416	58
Kennebec Co.	~	170	Walthall Co.	~	22
Maryland			Webster Co.	12	~
Baltimore City[b]	4,113	3,899	Winstonchoctaw Reg. Corr. Fac.	~	350
Charles Co. Det. Ctr.	377	~	**Missouri**		
Harford Co. Det. Ctr.	461	400	Arnold Municipal City[a]	~	7
Prince Georges Co. Corr. Ctr.	1,385	1,486	Belton City	10	~
Worcester Co.	253	~	Clay Co. Det. Ctr.	322	~
Massachusetts			Douglas Co.	~	19
Hampshire Co. Jail & House of Corr.[b]	288	~	Franklin Co.[b]	121	~
Norfolk Co.	~	702	Greene Co.[f]	539	~
Plymouth Co. House of Corr. & Jail	1,516	1,596	Jackson Co. Det. Ctr.	~	784
Michigan			Lincoln Co.[a,g]	~	147
Antrim Co.	40	~	Marion Co.	6	~
Bay Co. Law Enforcement Ctr.	~	219	Montgomery Co.	~	76
Benzie Co.	~	31	Ozark Co.	16	~
Calhoun Co.	497	~	St. Charles Co.	~	329
Cass Co.	~	126	Stoddard Co.	65	~
Emmet Co.	86	~	**Montana**		
Ingham Co.[b,f]	672	685	Cascade Co. Reg. Jail	380	~
Kalamazoo Co.[b]	324	365	Fallon Co.[a]	~	1
Kent Co.[a]	1,307	1,352	Flathead Co. Det. Ctr.[c]	~	92
Mecosta Co.	~	86	Missoula Co.	314	337
Monroe Co.	328	~	Pondera Co.	6	~
Saginaw Co.[a]	~	516	Sanders Co.	~	20
St. Clair Co.	428	408	**Nebraska**		
St. Joseph Co.	269	~	Box Butte Co.[b]	16	~
Wayne Co.[a]	2,185	2,713	Douglas Dept. of Corr.	1,148	1,041
Minnesota			Hamilton Co.	~	6
Anoka Co.	228	~	Harlan Co.	~	3
Beltrami Co.	~	121	Lancaster Co.	450	474
Dakota Co.	~	335	Morrill Co.	~	13
			Thayer Co.	3	~

Local jail authorities with no reported allegations of staff-on-inmate sexual victimization, 2007-2008

Jurisdiction and facility	Average daily population, 2008	Average daily population, 2007	Jurisdiction and facility	Average daily population, 2008	Average daily population, 2007
Nevada			**Ohio**		
North Las Vegas Det. Corr. Ctr.	~	869	Butler Co.	1,042	1,101
New Hampshire			Clermont Co.	304	~
Hillsborough Co. House of Corr.	583	~	Clinton Co.	19	~
Rockingham Co. Jail & House of Corr.	332	~	Crawford Co.	111	112
New Jersey			Delaware Co.	163	~
Bergen Co. Jail & Annex	~	970	Fayette Co.[b]	52	~
Burlington Co.	~	703	Greene Co.	~	381
Camden Co. Corr. Fac.	1,640	1,608	Hamilton Co.	2,019	2,086
Cumberland Co.	580	~	Lorain Co.	427	450
Gloucester Co.	373	~	Mahoning Co.	561	527
Somerset Co. Jail & Annex	~	324	Miami Co.[a]	~	104
New Mexico			Muskingum Co.	~	154
Catron Co.	~	4	Niles City	2	~
Curry Co.	37	~	Noble Co.	~	20
Dona Ana Co. Det. Ctr.	852	~	Richland Co.	~	152
Lea Co.	~	299	Summit Co. Jail & Glenwood Annex[b]	658	~
Luna Co.	~	392	**Oklahoma**		
Roosevelt Co.	79	~	Carter Co.	~	185
Sandoval Co.	396	~	Comanche Co.[a]	291	298
San Juan Co. Det. Ctr.	~	606	Grady Co.	334	~
New York			Latimer Co.	100	~
Albany Co. Corr. Fac.	687	762	Midwest City	~	48
Chenango Co.[b]	79	~	Muldrow City[a]	~	6
Erie Co. Holding Ctr.[b]	1,364	~	Muskogee Co. City Det. Ctr.	~	287
Erie Couny Corr. Fac.	~	1,469	Oklahoma Co.	2,281	2,369
Jefferson Co.	142	~	Roger Mills Co.	~	17
Madison Co.[b]	3	~	Rogers Co.[b]	192	~
Monroe Co.	1,343	1,450	Stephens Co.[a]	~	108
Montgomery Co.	~	126	Washington Co.[f]	102	91
Niagara Co.[d]	489	~	Woodward Co.	31	~
Oneida Co. Corr. Fac.	~	468	**Oregon**		
Onondaga Co. Dept. of Corr.	474	~	Marion Co.[b]	501	~
Rockland Co. Corr. Ctr.	~	262	Polk Co.	~	115
Schenectady Co.	305	317	**Pennsylvania**		
St. Lawrence Co.	~	112	Allegheny Co.[a]	2,749	2,650
Tioga Co.	~	83	Berks Co. Prison	1,109	1,304
North Carolina			Blair Co. Prison[d]	304	~
Buncombe Co.	409	475	Bucks Co.	780	1,180
Cabarrus Co.	~	217	Centre Co. Prison	~	212
Duplin Co.	~	16	Clearfield Co. Prison	135	~
Edgecombe Co.	282	260	Erie Co.	632	~
Forsyth Co.	891	~	Greene Co. Prison	~	105
Gaston Co.	541	517	Lebanon Co. Corr. Fac.[b]	518	538
Guilford Co.	~	926	Lehigh Co.	1,169	1,181
Lee Co.[a]	~	161	Washington Co.	413	~
McDowell Co.[b]	104	~	**South Carolina**		
Moore Co.	129	~	Abbeville Co. Det. Ctr.	61	~
Pamlico Co.	~	87	Aiken Co. Dt. Ctr.	422	~
Richmond Co.	86	87	Anderson Co.	428	~
Robeson Co.	377	~	Beaufort Co. Det. Ctr.	300	~
Rowan Co.	274	~	Berkeley Co. Det. Ctr.	~	362
Vance Co.	~	153	Charleston Co.[a,b]	1,694	1,762
Wake Co.	1,331	1,211	Horry Co. Det. Ctr.[b]	656	~
Wilson Co.[b]	220	~	Pickens Co.	~	96
North Dakota					
Grand Forks Co. Corr. Ctr.[b]	171	159			
Pembina Co.[f]	7	~			

Local jail authorities with no reported allegations of staff-on-inmate sexual victimization, 2007-2008

Jurisdiction and facility	Average daily population, 2008	Average daily population, 2007	Jurisdiction and facility	Average daily population, 2008	Average daily population, 2007
South Dakota			Wichita Co.[d]	435	435
Bon Homme Co.	~	6	Zavala Co.	9	~
Hughes Co.	48	~	**Utah**		
Meade Co.	~	45	Beaver Co.	370	~
Minnehaha Co.[a,b]	520	520	Cache Co.[a]	~	306
Pennington Co. Jail	420	~	Tooele Co.	~	119
Winner City[g]	~	63	Weber Co. Corr. Fac.[a]	973	770
Carroll Co.[b]	76	74	**Virginia**		
Greene Co.	366	~	Accomack Co.	~	113
Lawrence Co.	130	~	Albemarle-Charlottesville Reg. Jail[b]	520	538
Lincoln Co.	125	~	Alexandria City Det. Ctr.[b]	540	~
Madison Co. Penal Farm	~	80	Botetourt Co.[b]	91	~
Rutherford Co.	771	~	Central Virginia Reg. Jail	372	395
Shelby Co. Corr. Ctr.	2,960	2,960	Danville City	~	208
Sullivan Co.	675	584	Danville City Prison Farm[a,b]	149	164
Sumner Co.[a]	~	616	Middle River Reg. Jail	651	~
Warren Co.	212	~	Newport News City	629	~
Washington Co.[d,h]	519	~	Norfolk Municipal Jail	1,638	1,727
Williamson Co.[a,b]	311	341	Northern Neck Reg. Jail	451	~
Wilson Co.	~	250	Patrick Co.	27	~
Texas			Peumansend Creek Reg. Jail[a]	275	288
Angelina Co.	258	~	Rappahannock Co.	~	16
Bell Co. Law Enforcement Ctr.	672	~	Rappahannock Reg. Jail & Annex[b]	1,017	1,003
Brazos Co.	553	~	Roanoke Co.	286	~
Caldwell Co.	~	168	Rockingham Reg. Jail	~	295
Cameron Co.[a]	100	971	Virginia Peninsula Reg. Jail	~	489
Collin Co.	897	~	**Washington**		
Denton Co. Det. Ctr.	1,121	1,065	Asotin Co.	~	47
Ector Co.[a,b]	583	594	Benton Co.	672	~
Edwards Co.	9	~	Buckley City[b]	22	~
El Paso Co. Det. Fac.	2,209	2,220	Kent City[a]	~	139
Guadalupe Co. Det. Ctr.	378	460	Kirkland City	~	7
Hays Co.	315	~	Skagit Co.	237	~
Hidalgo Co. Adult Det. Ctr.[a,b]	1,132	1,185	Spokane Co. Geiger Corr. Ctr.	510	562
Hood Co.	161	~	Whatcom Co.	428	~
Jasper Co. Law Enforcement Ctr.	~	62	**West Virginia**		
Jefferson Co. Det. Ctr.[a]	924	1,176	Marshall Co. Northern Reg. Jail & Corr. Complex	~	314
Lipscomb Co.	~	2	North Central Reg. Jail	517	~
Lubbock Co.	724	1,000	Tygart Valley Reg. Jail	356	~
McLennan Co.	869	860	Western Reg. Jail[g]	~	461
Maverick Co.	~	230	**Wisconsin**		
Midland Co.[a]	~	280	Adams Co.	~	64
Mills Co.	7	~	Barron Co. Justice Ctr.	~	123
Montgomery Co.	815	1,112	Brown Co.[a]	~	770
Nueces Co.	950	~	Burnett Co. Law Enforcement Ctr.[b]	30	~
Parker Co.[b]	310	~	Dane Co.	926	~
Randall Co.	~	272	Dodge Co.	462	463
Rusk Co.[b]	89	88	Eau Claire Co.	~	274
San Patricio Co.	192	~	Ozaukee Co.	~	220
Shelby Co.	~	51	Racine Co.[b]	788	~
Sherman Co.[a]	~	2	Richland Co.	~	27
Tarrant Co.[c]	3,333	3,377	Rock Co.	~	521
Tom Green Co.	~	415	Shawano Co.[b]	510	~
Upton Co.	38	~	Waukesha Co.	655	~
Victoria Co.[b]	450	~			
Walker Co.	~	130			

Local jail authorities with no reported allegations of staff-on inmate sexual victimization, 2007-2008

Jurisdiction and facility	Average daily population, 2008	Average daily population, 2007
Wyoming		
Fremont Co.	~	166
Laramie Co.	222	~
Natrona Co. Det. Ctr.[a]	~	297
Platte Co.	97	~
Sheridan Co.	90	~
Sweetwater Co.[a]	~	119

~ Not applicable. Facility not sampled in survey year.

[a]Allegations of staff sexual harassment could not be counted separately from allegations of staff sexual misconduct in 2007.

[b]Allegations of staff sexual harassment could not be counted separately from allegations of staff sexual misconduct in 2008.

[c]Jurisdiction did not record allegations of staff sexual harassment in 2007.

[d]Jurisdiction did not record allegations of staff sexual harassment in 2008.

[e]Jurisdiction did not record allegations of staff sexual misconduct in 2007.

[f]Counts of staff sexual misconduct in 2008 are based on substantiated allegations only.

[g]Counts of staff sexual misconduct in 2007 are based on substantiated allegations only.

[h]Jurisdiction did not record allegations of staff sexual misconduct in 2008.

Allegations of inmate-on-inmate sexual victimization reported by private prison and jail authorities, by year and type of victimization, 2007-2008

Jurisdiction and facility	Average daily population (2008)	Reported inmate-on-inmate nonconsensual sexual acts (2008)		Reported inmate-on-inmate abusive sexual contacts (2008)		Average daily population (2007)	Reported inmate-on-inmate nonconsensual sexual acts (2007)		Reported inmate-on-inmate abusive sexual contacts (2007)	
		Allegations	Substantiated	Allegations	Substantiated		Allegations	Substantiated	Allegations	Substantiated
Total	/	56	6	14	4	/	58	6	27	0
Arizona										
Eloy Det. Ctr. (CCA)	1,456	0	0	1	0	1,449	3	0	1	0
Colorado										
Bent Co. Corr. Fac. (CCA)	847	1	0	1	0	~	~	~	~	~
High Plains Corr. Fac. (GRW/CCI)[a,b]	~	~	~	~	~	244	8	0	19	0
Florida										
Bay Corr. Inst. (CCA)	25	2	0	0	0	~	~	~	~	~
Lake City Corr. Fac.(CCA)	906	4	0	0	0	891	3	0	0	0
South Bay Corr. Fac. (GEO)[c]	1,858	4	0	/	/	~	~	~	~	~
Georgia										
Coffee Corr. Fac.(CCA)[c,d]	1,691	~	~	/	/	1,690	10	0	/	/
D. Ray James Prison	1,796	0	0	2	0	1,728	0	0	0	0
Wheeler Corr. Fac. (CCA)[d,e]	1,692	1	0	/	/	1,680	3	0	/	/
Idaho										
Idaho Corr. Fac. (CCA)[c]	1,493	0	0	/	/	1,464	0	0	1	0
Illinois										
Substance Abuse Services-Marion (FWHS)	39	0	0	1	0	~	~	~	~	~
Kansas										
Leavenworth Det. Ctr. (CCA)	1,057	1	0	0	0	962	0	0	0	0
Kentucky										
Lee Adjustment Ctr. (CCA)	684	2	0	0	0	~	~	~	~	~
Louisiana										
Allen Corr. Ctr. (GEO)[b]	1,469	0	0	0	0	1,530	2	0	0	0
Mississippi										
East Mississippi Corr. Fac.(GEO)	950	2	0	2	1	870	2	1	0	0
Tallahatchie Co. Corr. Fac. (CCA)	1,685	0	0	0	0	1,500	5	0	2	0
Walnut Grove Youth Corr. Fac. (CCI)	1,019	1	0	0	0	~	~	~	~	~
Montana										
Helena Pre-Release Ctr. (BACS)	92	1	1	0	0	~	~	~	~	~
New Mexico										
Lea Co. Corr. Fac. (GEO)[f]	1,238	1	0	0	0	1,240	0	0	0	0
Ohio										
Oriana House, Inc.	16	2	0	0	0	~	~	~	~	~
Oklahoma										
Cimarron Corr. Fac. (CCA)	993	5	2	0	0	1,021	6	3	0	0
David L. Moss Criminal Justice Ctr.[g]	1,425	1	1	3	3	1,517	0	0	0	0
Davis Corr. Fac.(CCA)	1,062	6	0	1	0	~	~	~	~	~
Diamondback Corr. Fac. (CCA)	2,150	1	0	0	0	2,093	0	0	0	0
Lawton Corr. Fac. (GEO)[e]	2,480	8	2	/	/	2,498	8	0	2	0
Tennessee										
Hardeman Co. Corr. Ctr. (CCA)	1,963	2	0	0	0	1,962	0	0	0	0
South Central Ctr. (CCA)	1,633	4	0	2	0	1,642	5	1	2	0
Whiteville Corr. Fac. (CCA)[c]	1,489	2	0	/	/	~	~	~	~	~
Texas										
Big Spring Corr. Ctr. (CCI)[c,d]	3,389	0	0	/	/	2,835	2	1	/	/
Bradshaw State Jail (CCA)[c]	1,970	3	0	/	/	~	~	~	~	~
Dalby Corr. Ctr. (MTC)	1,875	1	0	0	0	~	~	~	~	~
Eden Corr. Ctr. (CCA)	1,495	0	0	0	0	1,540	1	0	0	0

Allegations of inmate-on-inmate sexual victimization reported by private prison and jail authorities, by year and type of victimization, 2007-2008

Jurisdiction and facility	2008 Average daily population	2008 Reported inmate-on-inmate nonconsensual sexual acts		2008 Reported inmate-on-inmate abusive sexual contacts		2007 Average daily population	2007 Reported inmate-on-inmate nonconsensual sexual acts		2007 Reported inmate-on-inmate abusive sexual contacts	
		Allegations	Substantiated	Allegations	Substantiated		Allegations	Substantiated	Allegations	Substantiated
Virginia										
Lawrenceville Corr. Ctr. (GEO)	1,557	1	0	1	0	1,554	0	0	0	0

--Not applicable.

/Not reported.

BACS—Boyd Andrew Community Services

CCA—Corrections Corp. of America

CCI—Cornell Companies, Inc.

FWHS—Franklin-Williamson Human Services, Inc.

GEO—The GEO Group, Inc.

MTC—Management & Training Corp.

SMBH—Southeast Missouri Behavioral Health

[a]Cornell Companies, Inc. took over management of the Brush Correctional Facility from GRW Corporation in May 2007. It was renamed High Plains Correctional Facility.

[b]Counts of nonconsensual sexual acts in 2007 are based on substantiated allegations only.

[c]Allegations of abusive sexual contacts could not be counted separately from allegations of nonconsensual sexual acts in 2008.

[d]Allegations of abusive sexual contacts could not be counted separately from allegations of nonconsensual sexual acts in 2007.

[e]Facility did not record allegations of abusive sexual contact in 2008.

[f]Counts of nonconsensual sexual acts in 2008 are based on completed acts only.

[g]Facility is currently operated locally.

Private prison and jail authorities with no reported allegations of inmate-on-inmate sexual victimization, 2007-2008

Jurisdiction and facility	Average daily population, 2008	Average daily population, 2007
Arizona		
Arizona State Prison - Florence West (GEO)	698	~
Arizona State Prison - Kingman (MTC)	1,490	~
Arizona State Prison - Phoenix West (GEO)	479	512
California		
California City Corr. Ctr. (CCA)[a,b]	2,621	692
Central Valley Community Corr. Fac. (GEO)	585	600
Desert View Community Corr. Fac. (GEO)	584	~
Taft Corr. Inst. (MTC)[a]	2,355	2,316
Colorado		
Crowley Co. Corr. Fac.(CCA)[c]	1,630	~
Kit Carson Co. Corr. Ctr. (CCA)	960	749
Phoenix Ctr. Adams Co. Community Corr. (CEC)[c]	228	~
Tooley Hall (CEC)	59	~
Women's Remediation Ctr. (CC)[c]	308	~
Connecticut		
Berman Treatment Ctr. (CSI)	17	~
Florida		
Citrus Co. Det. Fac. (CCA)	646	~
Gadsden Corr. Fac. (CCA)	137	1,273
Hillsborough Co. (CSC)	92	~
Moore Haven Corr. Fac. (GEO)	15	~
McRae Corr. Fac. (CCA)	1,724	~
Illinois		
Southwood Interventions (CCI)[a]	~	101
Kentucky		
Dismas Charities-Portland (DCI)	218	~
Marion Adjustment Ctr. (CCA)[a]	~	790
Louisiana		
C.I.N.C., Inc.	180	~
Winn Corr. Ctr. (CCA)	1,461	~
Minnesota		
Prairie Corr. Fac. (CCA)[c]	1,413	~
Mississippi		
Delta Corr. Fac.(CCA)	968	970
Wilkinson Co. Corr. Ctr.(CCA)	988	~
Missouri		
S.E. Missouri Comm. Treatment Ctr. (SMBH)[c]	38	~
Montana		
Alpha House (AI)[c]	158	~

Jurisdiction and facility	Average daily population, 2008	Average daily population, 2007
New Jersey		
Bo Robinson Education & Training Ctr. (CEC)	~	495
Hope Hall (VOA)[c]	170	~
Talbot Hall (CEC)	499	~
New Mexico		
Cibola Co. Corr. Ctr. (CCA)	1,138	~
Dismas Charities - Las Cruces (DCI)	73	~
New Mexico Women's Corr. Fac. (CCA)[c]	563	576
Valencia Co. Adult Det. Ctr. - Cornell Corr.	~	163
North Carolina		
Rivers Corr. Inst. (GEO)	1,298	~
Ohio		
Alvis House Cope Ctr.[e]	~	22
Lake Erie Corr. Inst. (MTC)	1,484	~
N.E. Ohio Corr. Ctr. (CCA)	1,982	~
North Coast Corr. Treatment Fac. (MTC)	~	649
Oklahoma		
Carver Corr. Ctr. (ACS)	277	~
Catalyst Behavioral Services - Ivanhoe	102	92
Great Plains Corr. Fac. (CCI)	1,153	~
Pennsylvania		
Kintock - Philadelphia	338	337
Tennessee		
Salvation Army Ctr.	47	~
Texas		
B.M. Moore Corr. Ctr. (MTC)	499	~
Bartlett (CCA)	1,046	1,003
Bridgeport Corr. Ctr. (GEO)	519	518
Bridgeport PPT (CCA)	200	~
Country Rehab. Ctr., Inc. of Tyler	~	46
Dawson State Jail (CCA)	2,188	2,182
Estes Unit (MTC)	1,036	~
Kyle Unit (CEC)	519	~
Liberty Co. Jail (CEC)	318	~
Limestone Co. Det. Ctr. (CEC)[c]	1,005	997
Lindsey State Jail (CCA)	1,027	~
Lockhart PPT (GEO)	~	997
Mineral Wells PPT (CCA)	2,056	2,085
Reeves Co. Det. Ctr. (GEO)[c,f]	2,175	2,147
Reeves Co. Det. Ctr. III	1,350	~
Willacy Co. State Jail (CCA)	1,065	1,059

ACS—Avalon Correctional Services, Inc.
AI—Alternatives, Inc.
CC—ComCor, Inc.
CCA—Corrections Corp. of America
CCI—Cornell Companies, Inc.

CEC—Community Education Centers, Inc.
CSC—Correctional Services Corp.
CSI—Community Solutions, Inc.
DCI—Dismas Charities, Inc.
GEO—The GEO Group, Inc.

MTC—Management & Training Corp.
SMBH—Southeast Missouri Behavioral Health
VOA—Volunteers of America - Delaware Valley

~Not applicable.

[a]Allegations of abusive sexual contacts could not be counted separately from allegations of nonconsensual sexual acts in 2007.

[b]Facility did not record allegations of abusive sexual contact in 2008.

[c]Allegations of abusive sexual contacts could not be counted separately from allegations of nonconsensual sexual acts in 2008.

[d]Facility is currently closed.

[e]Counts of nonconsensual sexual acts in 2007 are based on substantiated allegations only.

[f]Counts of nonconsensual sexual acts in 2008 are based on substantiated allegations only.

Allegations of staff-on-inmate sexual victimization reported by private prison and jail authorities, by year and type of victimization, 2007-2008

Jurisdiction and facility	2008					2007				
	Average daily population	Reported allegations of staff sexual misconduct with inmates		Reported allegations of staff sexual harassment of inmates		Average daily population	Reported allegations of staff sexual misconduct with inmates		Reported allegations of staff sexual harassment of inmates	
		Allegations	Substantiated	Allegations	Substantiated		Allegations	Substantiated	Allegations	Substantiated
Total	/	59	20	8	1	/	29	7	5	0
Arizona										
Eloy Det. Ctr. (CCA)	1,456	2	0	0	0	1,449	1	0	0	0
California										
Taft Corr. Inst. (MTC)[a]	2,355	1	0	0	0	2,316	0	0	/	/
Colorado										
Crowley Co. Corr. Fac.(CCA)	1,630	4	0	0	0	~	~	~	~	~
High Plains Corr. Fac. (GRW/CCI)[b,c]	~	~	~	~	~	244	1	0	0	0
Kit Carson Co. Corr. Ctr. (CCA)	960	0	0	0	0	749	4	0	1	0
Florida										
Gadsden Corr. Fac. (CCA)	137	3	1	0	0	1,273	0	0	0	0
Lake City Corr. Fac.(CCA)	906	1	0	0	0	891	1	1	0	0
Moore Haven Corr. Fac. (GEO)[d]	15	1	0	/	/	~	~	~	~	~
South Bay Corr. Fac. (GEO)	1,858	1	1	0	0	~	~	~	~	~
Georgia										
Coffee Corr. Fac.(CCA)	1,691	1	0	1	0	1,690	0	0	0	0
D. Ray James Prison[a]	1,796	3	0	1	0	1,728	0	0	/	/
McRae Corr. Fac. (CCA)	1,724	1	1	0	0	~	~	~	~	~
Idaho										
Idaho Corr. Fac. (CCA)	1,493	1	0	0	0	1,464	1	0	0	0
Illinois										
Substance Abuse Services-Marion (FWHS)	39	2	0	0	0	~	~	~	~	~
Kansas										
Leavenworth Det. Ctr. (CCA)	1,057	2	1	0	0	962	0	0	0	0
Kentucky										
Lee Adjustment Ctr. (CCA)	684	4	1	0	0	~	~	~	~	~
Marion Adjustment Ctr. (CCA)[a]	~	~	~	~	~	790	2	1	/	/
Louisiana										
Winn Corr. Ctr. (CCA)	1,461	3	3	0	0	~	~	~	~	~
Minnesota										
Prairie Corr. Fac. (CCA)[d]	1,413	1	1	/	/	~	~	~	~	~
Mississippi										
Delta Corr. Fac.(CCA)	968	1	0	0	0	970	1	1	2	0
Marshall Co. Corr. Fac. (GEO)[e]	900	1	0	0	0	~	~	~	~	~
Wilkinson Co. Corr. Ctr.(CCA)	988	2	0	2	0	~	~	~	~	~
New Mexico										
New Mexico Women's Corr. Fac. (CCA)	563	4	0	1	1	576	0	0	0	0
North Carolina										
Rivers Corr. Inst. (GEO)	1,298	1	0	0	0	~	~	~	~	~
Ohio										
Lake Erie Corr. Inst. (MTC)	1,484	1	0	0	0	~	~	~	~	~
N.E. Ohio Corr. Ctr. (CCA)	1,982	1	0	0	0	~	~	~	~	~
Oklahoma										
Catalyst Behavioral Services - Ivanhoe	102	0	0	0	0	92	1	0	0	0
David L. Moss Criminal Justice Ctr.[a,f]	1,425	1	1	0	0	1,517	2	0	/	/
Diamondback Corr. Fac. (CCA)	2,150	2	2	0	0	2,093	2	2	1	0
Lawton Corr. Fac. (GEO)[d]	2,480	1	0	/	/	2,498	2	0	0	0
Pennsylvania										
Kintock - Philadelphia[d]	338	0	0	/	/	337	2	0	0	0
Tennessee										
South Central Ctr. (CCA)	1,633	3	1	0	0	1,642	2	1	0	0
Whiteville Corr. Fac. (CCA)	1,489	1	1	0	0	~	~	~	~	~

Allegations of staff-on-inmate sexual victimization reported by private prison and jail authorities, by year and type of victimization, 2007-2008

| | 2008 | | | | | 2007 | | | | |
| | Average daily population | Reported allegations of staff sexual misconduct with inmates | | Reported allegations of staff sexual harassment of inmates | | Average daily population | Reported allegations of staff sexual misconduct with inmates | | Reported allegations of staff sexual harassment of inmates | |
Jurisdiction and facility		Allegations	Substantiated	Allegations	Substantiated		Allegations	Substantiated	Allegations	Substantiated
Texas										
Big Spring Corr. Ctr. (CCI)a	3,389	3	3	0	0	2,835	2	1	/	/
Eden Corr. Ctr. (CCA)	1,495	2	1	0	0	1,540	0	0	0	0
Liberty Co. Jail (CEC)	318	2	2	0	0	~	~	~	~	~
Virginia										
Lawrenceville Corr. Ctr. (GEO)	1,557	2	0	3	0	1,554	5	0	1	0

~Not applicable.

/Not reported.

CCA—Corrections Corp. of America

CCI—Cornell Companies, Inc.

CEC—Community Education Centers, Inc.

GEO—The GEO Group, Inc.

aAllegations of staff sexual harassment could not be counted separately from allegations of staff sexual misconduct in 2007.

bCornell Companies, Inc. took over management of the Brush Correctional Facility from GRW Corporation in May 2007. It was renamed High Plains Correctional Facility.

cCounts of staff sexual misconduct in 2007 are based on substantiated allegations only.

dAllegations of staff sexual harassment could not be counted separately from allegations of staff sexual misconduct in 2008.

eFacility is currently closed.

fFacility is currently operated locally.

Private prison and jail authorities with no reported allegations of staff-on-inmate sexual victimization, 2007-2008

Jurisdiction and facility	Average daily population, 2008	Average daily population, 2007
Arizona		
Arizona State Prison - Florence West (GEO)	698	~
Arizona State Prison - Kingman (MTC)	1,490	~
Arizona State Prison - Phoenix West (GEO)	479	512
California		
California City Corr. Ctr. (CCA)	2,621	692
Central Valley Community Corr. Fac. (GEO)	585	600
Desert View Community Corr. Fac. (GEO)	584	~
Colorado		
Bent Co. Corr. Fac. (CCA)	847	~
Phoenix Ctr. Adams Co. Comm. Corr. (CEC)[a]	228	~
Tooley Hall (CEC)	59	~
Women's Remediation Ctr. (CC)	308	~
Connecticut		
Berman Treatment Ctr. (CSI)	17	~
Florida		
Bay Corr. Inst. (CCA)	25	~
Citrus Co. Det. Fac. (CCA)	646	~
Hillsborough Co. (CSC)	92	~
Georgia		
Wheeler Corr. Fac. (CCA)[a,b]	1,692	1,680
Illinois		
Southwood Interventions (CCI)[b]	~	101
Kentucky		
Dismas Charities-Portland (DCI)	218	~
Louisiana		
Allen Corr. Ctr. (GEO)	1,469	1,530
C.I.N.C., Inc.	180	~
Mississippi		
East Mississippi Corr. Fac.(GEO)	950	870
Tallahatchie Co. Corr. Fac. (CCA)	1,685	1,500
Walnut Grove Youth Corr. Fac. (CCI)	1,019	~
Missouri		
Southeast Missouri Comm. Treatment Ctr. (SMBH)	38	~
Montana		
Alpha House (AI)[a]	158	~
Helena Pre-Release Ctr. (BACS)[a]	92	~
New Jersey		
Bo Robinson Education & Training Ctr. (CEC)[b]	~	495
Hope Hall (VOA)	170	~
Talbot Hall (CEC)	499	~
New Mexico		
Cibola Co. Corr. Ctr (CCA)	1,138	~
Dismas Charities-Las Cruces (DCI)	73	~
Lea Co. Corr. Fac. (GEO)	1,238	1,240
Valencia Co. Adult Det. Ctr. - Cornell Corr.	~	163
Ohio		
Alvis House Cope Ctr.	~	22
North Coast Corr. Treatment Fac. (MTC)	~	649
Oriana House, Inc.	16	~
Oklahoma		
Carver Corr. Ctr. (ACS)[a,c]	277	~
Cimarron Corr. Fac. (CCA)	993	1,021
Davis Corr. Fac.(CCA)	1,062	~
Great Plains Corr. Fac. (CCI)	1,153	~
Pennsylvania		
George W. Hill Corr. Fac. (CEC)	~	1,877
Tennessee		
Hardeman Co. Corr. Ctr. (CCA)	1,963	1,962
Salvation Army Ctr.	47	~
Texas		
B.M. Moore Corr. Ctr. (MTC)	499	~
Bartlett (CCA)	1,046	1,003
Bradshaw State Jail (CCA)[a]	1,970	~
Bridgeport PPT (CCA)	519	518
Country Rehab. Ctr., Inc. of Tyler[b]	~	46
Dalby Corr. Ctr. (MTC)	1,875	~
Dawson State Jail (CCA)	2,188	2,182
Estes Unit (MTC)	1,036	~
Houston/Reid Facility (CCI)[a]	306	~
Kyle Unit (CEC)	519	~
Limestone Co. Det. Ctr. (CEC)[a]	1,005	997
Lindsey State Jail (CCA)	1,027	~
Lockhart PPT (GEO)	~	997
Mineral Wells PPT (CCA)	2,056	2,085
Reeves Co. Det. Ctr. (GEO)	2,175	2,147
Reeves Co. Det. Ctr. III	1,350	~
Willacy Co. State Jail (CCA)	1,065	1,059

ACS—Avalon Correctional Services, Inc.
AI—Alternatives, Inc.
BACS—Boyd Andrew Community Services
CC—ComCor, Inc.
CCA—Corrections Corp. of America

CCI—Cornell Companies, Inc.
CEC—Community Education Centers, Inc
CSC—Correctional Services Corp.
CSI—Community Solutions, Inc.
DCI—Dismas Charities, Inc.

GEO—The GEO Group, Inc.
MTC—Management & Training Corp.
SMBH—Southeast Missouri Behavioral Health
VOA—Volunteers of America - Delaware Valley

~Not applicable.

[a]Allegations of staff sexual harassment could not be counted separately from allegations of staff sexual misconduct in 2008.

[b]Allegations of staff sexual harassment could not be counted separately from allegations of staff sexual misconduct in 2007.

[c]Counts of staff sexual misconduct in 2008 are based on substantiated allegations only.

Allegations of inmate-on-inmate sexual victimization reported in other correctional facilties, by year and type of victimization, 2007-2008

Jurisdiction and facility	2008					2007				
	Average daily population	Reported inmate-on-inmate nonconsensual sexual acts		Reported inmate-on-inmate abusive sexual contacts		Average daily population	Reported inmate-on-inmate nonconsensual sexual acts		Reported inmate-on-inmate abusive sexual contacts	
		Allegations	Substantiated	Allegations	Substantiated		Allegations	Substantiated	Allegations	Substantiated
U.S. Military										
Total	1,798	1	0	1	1	1,844	0	0	1	0
Air Force	40	0	0	0	0	53	0	0	0	0
Army	811	1	0	0	0	974	0	0	0	0
Marines	431	0	0	0	0	381	0	0	1	0
Navy	516	0	0	1	1	436	0	0	0	0
U.S. Immigration and Customs Enforcement										
ICE - Florence (AZ)[a]	607	0	0	/	/	543	0	0	0	0
ICE - El Centro (CA)[a,b]	470	0	0	/	/	454	0	0	/	/
ICE - San Diego (CA)	662	1	0	0	0	671	1	0	0	0
ICE - Aurora (CO)	388	1	1	0	0	397	0	0	0	0
ICE - Broward Transitional Ctr. (FL)	581	0	0	0	0	.	.	.	.	.
ICE - Miami (FL)	~	~	~	~	~	677	0	0	0	0
ICE - Stewart Det. Ctr. (GA)[a]	1,670	0	0	/	/	~	~	~	~	~
ICE - Elizabeth (NJ)	258	0	0	0	0	270	0	0	0	0
ICE - Batavia (NY)	554	0	0	0	0	504	0	0	0	0
ICE - Varick Federal Det. Fac. (NY)	225	0	0	0	0	~	~	~	~	~
ICE - Aguadilla (PR)	~	~	~			40	0	0	0	0
ICE - El Paso (TX)[b]	800	0	0	0	0	800	0	0	/	/
ICE - Houston (TX)[c]	836	0	0	0	0	853	0	0	0	0
ICE - Laredo (TX)	341	0	0	0	0	369	0	0	0	0
ICE - Port Isabel Service Processing Ctr. (TX)	700	0	0	0	0	~	~	~	~	~
ICE - South Texas Det. Fac. (TX)	1,803	0	0	0	0	~	~	~	~	~
ICE - Willacy Det. Ctr. (TX)	1,451	1	0	0	0	~	~	~	~	~
ICE - Tacoma (WA)[a]	956	0	0	/	/	980	0	0	0	0
Jails in Indian Country										
Colorado River Indian Tribes Adult Det. Ctr. (AZ)	~	~	~	~	~	38	0	0	0	0
Gila River Dept. of Rehab. & Supervision - Adult (AZ)	167	0	0	0	0	186	0	0	0	0
Navajo Nation - Chinle (AZ)[a]	27	0	0	/	/	~	~	~	~	~
Navajo Nation - Kayenta Police Dept. & Holding Fac. (AZ)	~	~	~	~	~	7	0	0	0	0
Navajo Nation - Shiprock Police Dept. & Adult Det. (AZ)[a]	77	0	0	/	/	~	~	~	~	~
Navajo Nation - Window Rock Adult Det. (AZ)	~	~	~	~	~	21	0	0	0	0
Salt River Pima- Maricopa Dept. of Corr. - Adult & Juv. (AZ)	~	~	~	~	~	65	0	0	0	0
San Carlos Dept. of Corr. & Rehabilitation - Adult (AZ)	107	0	0	0	0	1,284	0	0	0	0
Supai Law Enforcement & Holding Fac. (AZ)	~	~	~	~	~	0	0	0	0	0
Tohono O'Odham Tribe Adult Det. Ctr. (AZ)	145	0	0	0	0	145	0	0	0	0
Truxton Canyon Adult Det. Ctr. (AZ)	~	~	~	~	~	102	0	0	0	0
White Mountain Apache Det. Ctr. (AZ)	65	0	0	0	0	65	0	0	0	0
Chief Ignacio Justice Ctr. Adult Det. (CO)	~	~	~	~	~	41	0	0	0	0
Fort Hall Police Dept. & Adult Det. Ctr. (ID)	~	~	~	~	~	19	0	0	0	0
Saginaw Chippewa Tribal Police Dept. & Adult Det. Ctr. (MI)	~	~	~	~	~	0	0	0	0	0
Red Lake Tribal Justice Ctr. Adult Det. (MN)	~	~	~	~	~	38	0	0	0	0
Choctaw Justice Complex Adult Det. (MS)	~	~	~	~	~	35	0	0	0	0
Blackfeet Adult Det. Ctr. (MT)	~	~	~	~	~	22	0	0	0	0
Crow Adult Det. Ctr. (MT)	~	~	~	~	~	7	0	0	0	0
Flathead Adult Det. Ctr. (MT)[b]	~	~	~	~	~	4	0	0	/	/
Fort Peck Police Dept. & Adult Det. Ctr. (MT)	28	0	0	0	0	~	~	~	~	~
Northern Cheyenne Adult Det. Ctr. (MT)	~	~	~	~	~	35	0	0	0	0
Omaha Tribal Police Dept. & Adult Det. (MT)	~	~	~	~	~	22	0	0	0	0
Acoma Tribal Police & Holding Fac. (NM)	~	~	~	~	~	3	0	0	0	0
Jicarilla Apache Police Dept. (NM)	~	~	~	~	~	27	0	0	0	0
Navajo Nation - Crownpoint Adult Det. (NM)	~	~	~	~	~	14	0	0	0	0
Navajo Nation - Shiprock Police Dept. & Adult Det. (NM)	~	~	~	~	~	36	0	0	0	0
Zuni Adult Det. Ctr. (NM)	~	~	~	~	~	23	0	0	0	0
Fort Totten L.E. & Adult Det. Ctr. (ND)	~	~	~	~	~	4	0	0	0	0
Gerald Tex Fox Justice Ctr. Adult Det. (ND)	~	~	~	~	~	5	0	0	0	0
Standing Rock L.E. & Adult Det. (ND)	45	0	0	0	0	~	~	~	~	~

Allegations of inmate-on-inmate sexual victimization reported in other correctional facilties, by year and type of victimization, 2007-2008

Jurisdiction and facility	2008					2007				
	Average daily population	Reported inmate-on-inmate nonconsensual sexual acts		Reported inmate-on-inmate abusive sexual contacts		Average daily population	Reported inmate-on-inmate nonconsensual sexual acts		Reported inmate-on-inmate abusive sexual contacts	
		Allegations	Substantiated	Allegations	Substantiated		Allegations	Substantiated	Allegations	Substantiated
Jails in Indian Country (continued)										
Turtle Mountain L.E. & Adult Det. (ND)[a]	25	0	0	/	/	~	~	~	~	~
Warm Springs Police Dept. & Adult Det. Ctr. (OR)	51	0	0	0	0	53	0	0	0	0
Cheyenne River Sioux Adult Det. Ctr. (SD)	~	~	~	~	~	8	0	0	0	0
Kyle Police Dept. & Adult Det. (SD)[b]	~	~	~	~	~	35	0	0	/	/
Lower Brule Justice Ctr. - Adult Det. (SD)	~	~	~	~	~	5	0	0	0	0
Oglala Sioux Tribal Offenders Fac. (SD)	~	~	~	~	~	85	0	0	0	0
Rosebud Sioux Tribe Police Dept. & Adult Det. (SD)	~	~	~	~	~	56	0	0	0	0
Chehalis Tribal Police Dept. & Adult Det. Ctr. (WA)	~	~	~	~	~	10	0	0	0	0
Colville Adult Det. Ctr. (WA)	30	0	0	0	0	46	0	0	0	0
Makah Public Safety-Adult Det. (WA)	~	~	~	~	~	4	0	0	0	0
Nisqually Adult Corrections (WA)[a]	57	0	0	/	/	65	0	0	0	0
Puyallup Tribal Law Enforcement & Adult Det. (WA)[b]	~	~	~	~	~	8	0	0	/	/
Quinault Nation Police Dept. & Holding Fac. (WA)	~	~	~	~	~	2	0	0	0	0
Spokane Adult Det. Ctr. (WA)	~	~	~	~	~	17	0	0	0	0
Menominee Police Dept. & Det. Ctr. (WI)	~	~	~	~	~	48	0	0	0	0
Wind River Adult Det. Ctr. (WY)	15	0	0	0	0	15	0	0	0	0

~Not applicable.

/Not reported.

[a]Allegations of abusive sexual contacts could not be counted separately from allegations of nonconsensual sexual acts in 2008.

[b]Allegations of abusive sexual contacts could not be counted separately from allegations of nonconsensual sexual acts in 2007.

[c]Counts of nonconsensual sexual acts in 2008 are based on substantiated allegations only.

Allegations of staff-on-inmate sexual victimization reported in other correctional facilties, by year and type of victimization, 2007-2008

	2008				2007			
	Reported allegations of staff sexual misconduct with inmates		Reported allegations of staff sexual harassment of inmates		Reported allegations of staff sexual misconduct with inmates		Reported allegations of staff sexual harassment of inmates	
Jurisdiction and facility	Allegations	Substantiated	Allegations	Substantiated	Allegations	Substantiated	Allegations	Substantiated
U.S. Military								
Total	4	4	0	0	2	1	0	0
Air Force	0	0	0	0	0	0	0	0
Army	4	4	0	0	1	1	0	0
Marines	0	0	0	0	0	0	0	0
Navy	0	0	0	0	1	0	0	0
U.S. Immigration and Customs Enforcement								
ICE - Florence (AZ)	0	0	0	0	0	0	0	0
ICE - El Centro (CA)[a,b]	0	0	/	/	0	0	/	/
ICE - San Diego (CA)	0	0	0	0	1	1	0	0
ICE - Aurora (CO)	0	0	0	0	0	0	0	0
ICE - Broward Transitional Ctr. (FL)	0	0	0	0	~	~	~	~
ICE - Miami (FL)	~	~	~	~	0	0	0	0
ICE - Stewart Det. Ctr. (GA)[b]	0	0	/	/	~	~	~	~
ICE - Elizabeth (NJ)	1	0	1	0	0	0	0	0
ICE - Batavia (NY)	0	0	0	0	0	0	0	0
ICE - Varick Federal Det. Fac. (NY)	0	0	0	0	~	~	~	~
ICE - Aguadilla (PR)[a]	~	~	~	~	0	0	/	/
ICE - El Paso (TX)	0	0	0	0	0	0	1	0
ICE - Houston (TX)[c]	0	0	0	0	0	0	0	0
ICE - Laredo (TX)	0	0	1	0	1	0	0	0
ICE - Port Isabel Service Processing Ctr. (TX)	0	0	0	0	~	~	~	~
ICE - South Texas Det. Fac. (TX)	0	0	0	0	~	~	~	~
ICE - Willacy Det. Ctr. (TX)	0	0	0	0	~	~	~	~
ICE - Tacoma (WA)	0	0	0	0	0	0	0	0
Jails in Indian Country								
Colorado River Indian Tribes Adult Det. Ctr. (AZ)	~	~	~	~	0	0	0	0
Gila River Dept. of Rehab. & Supervision - Adult (AZ)	1	1	1	1	0	0	0	0
Navajo Nation - Chinle (AZ)[b]	0	0	/	/	~	~	~	~
Navajo Nation - Kayenta Police Dept. & Holding Fac. (AZ)[a]	~	~	~	~	0	0	/	/
Navajo Nation - Shiprock Police Dept. & Adult Det. (AZ)[b]	0	0	/	/	~	~	~	~
Navajo Nation - Window Rock Adult Det. (AZ)	~	~	~	~	0	0	0	0
Salt River Pima-Maricopa Dept. of Corr. - Adult & Juv. (AZ)	~	~	~	~	0	0	0	0
San Carlos Dept. of Corr. & Rehabilitation - Adult (AZ)	0	0	0	0	0	0	0	0
Supai Law Enforcement & Holding Fac. (AZ)	~	~	~	~	0	0	0	0
Tohono O'Odham Tribe Adult Det. Ctr. (AZ)	0	0	0	0	0	0	0	0
Truxton Canyon Adult Det. Ctr. (AZ)	~	~	~	~	0	0	0	0
White Mountain Apache Det. Ctr. (AZ)	0	0	0	0	0	0	0	0
Chief Ignacio Justice Ctr. Adult Det. (CO)	~	~	~	~	0	0	0	0
Fort Hall Police Dept. & Adult Det. Ctr. (ID)	~	~	~	~	1	0	0	0
Saginaw Chippewa Tribal Police Dept. & Adult Det Ctr. (MI)	~	~	~	~	0	0	0	0
Red Lake Tribal Justice Ctr. Adult Det. (MN)	~	~	~	~	0	0	0	0
Choctaw Justice Complex Adult Det. (MS)	~	~	~	~	2	2	0	0
Blackfeet Adult Det. Ctr. (MT)	~	~	~	~	0	0	0	0
Crow Adult Det. Ctr. (MT)	~	~	~	~	0	0	0	0
Flathead Adult Det. Ctr. (MT)[a]	~	~	~	~	0	0	/	/
Fort Peck Police Dept. & Adult Det. Ctr. (MT)	0	0	0	0	~	~	~	~
Northern Cheyenne Adult Det. Ctr. (MT)	~	~	~	~	0	0	0	0
Omaha Tribal Police Dept. & Adult Det. (MT)	~	~	~	~	0	0	0	0
Acoma Tribal Police & Holding Fac. (NM)	~	~	~	~	0	0	0	0
Jicarilla Apache Police Dept. (NM)	~	~	~	~	0	0	0	0
Navajo Nation - Crownpoint Adult Det. (NM)	~	~	~	~	1	0	0	0
Navajo Nation - Shiprock Police Dept. & Adult Det. (NM)	~	~	~	~	0	0	0	0

Allegations of staff-on-inmate sexual victimization reported in other correctional facilties, by year and type of victimization, 2007-2008

	2008				2007			
	Reported allegations of staff sexual misconduct with inmates		Reported allegations of staff sexual harassment of inmates		Reported allegations of staff sexual misconduct with inmates		Reported allegations of staff sexual harassment of inmates	
Jurisdiction and facility	Allegations	Substantiated	Allegations	Substantiated	Allegations	Substantiated	Allegations	Substantiated
Jails in Indian Country (continued)								
Zuni Adult Det. Ctr. (NM)	~	~	~	~	0	0	0	0
Fort Totten L.E. & Adult Det. Ctr. (ND)[a]	~	~	~	~	0	0	/	/
Gerald Tex Fox Justice Ctr. Adult Det. (ND)	~	~	~	~	0	0	0	0
Standing Rock L.E. & Adult Det. (ND)	0	0	0	0	~	~	~	~
Turtle Mountain L.E. Adult Det. (ND)	0	0	0	0	~	~	~	~
Warm Springs Police Dept. & Adult Det. Ctr. (OR)	0	0	0	0	1	0	0	0
Cheyenne River Sioux Adult Det. Ctr. (SD)	~	~	~	~	0	0	0	0
Kyle Police Dept. & Adult Det. (SD)[a]	~	~	~	~	0	0	/	/
Lower Brule Justice Ctr. - Adult Det. (SD)	~	~	~	~	0	0	0	0
Oglala Sioux Tribal Offenders Fac. (SD)	~	~	~	~	1	1	0	0
Rosebud Sioux Tribe Police Dept. & Adult Det. (SD)	~	~	~	~	0	0	0	0
Chehalis Tribal Police Dept. & Adult Det. Ctr. (WA)	~	~	~	~	0	0	0	0
Colville Adult Det. Ctr. (WA)	0	0	0	0	0	0	0	0
Makah Public Safety-Adult Det. (WA)	~	~	~	~	2	2	1	1
Nisqually Adult Corrections (WA)	0	0	0	0	0	0	0	0
Puyallup Tribal Law Enforcement & Adult Det. (WA)[a]	~	~	~	~	0	0	/	/
Quinault Nation Police Dept. & Holding Fac. (WA)	~	~	~	~	0	0	0	0
Spokane Adult Det. Ctr. (WA)	~	~	~	~	0	0	0	0
Menominee Police Dept. & Det. Ctr. (WI)	~	~	~	~	0	0	0	0
Wind River Adult Det. Ctr. (WY)	0	0	0	0	0	0	0	0

~Not applicable.

/Not reported.

[a]Allegations of staff sexual harassment could not be counted separately from allegations of staff sexual misconduct in 2007.

[b]Allegations of staff sexual harassment could not be counted separately from allegations of staff sexual misconduct in 2008.

[c]Counts of staff sexual misconduct in 2008 are based on substantiated allegations only.

www.ingramcontent.com/pod-product-compliance
Lightning Source LLC
Chambersburg PA
CBHW080544290526
45790CB00006B/2548